Towers in the City

I0809234

LEXITY
FÜR BERLIN. WAS
FÜR EINE FLOT

Towers in the City

Berlin Alexanderplatz

Edited by Kyle Dugdale with Kirk Henderson

Yale School of Architecture

Hans Kollhoff, Davenport Visiting Professor
Kyle Dugdale, Critic in Architecture

Yale School of Architecture

Printed and bound in the United States of America

ISBN 978-1-638409021

Publisher
Yale School of Architecture
180 York Street
New Haven, CT 06511
www.architecture.yale.edu

This book was published through the Dean's office.
All texts by Hans Kollhoff are reprinted by permission of the author.

Distributor
Actar
440 Park Avenue South
New York, NY 10016
www.actar.com

Editors
Kyle Dugdale
Kirk Henderson

Publications Director
Nina Rappaport

frontispiece Philipp Schaefer, Bernhard-Weiß-Straße 6 (previously Neue Königstraße 27), 1931. Once Berlin's largest office building, what was then the administrative headquarters of Karstadt is now the Senate Department for Education, Youth and Family. Schaefer's vertically-articulated structures of the period rival contemporary skscrapers in New York and Chicago. His best-known building was Berlin's Karstadt department store of 1927, the most modern in Europe.

Contents

We are living in a world of products that were all up-to-date, once, for a moment—but that suddenly become obsolete and fall into rapid decay. You cannot build a house with such things, and most certainly not a city.[1]

[1] Hans Kollhoff, "Markt und Werk," *Deutsches Architektur-Museum Architektur Jahrbuch* (1994): 9; translated by Kyle Dugdale.

above Hans Kollhoff, studio presentation, Berlin, January 13, 2016

Preface

Hans Kollhoff

If we want to create an urban fabric that we will want to live with for a long time, one which will express a collective feeling and which future generations will be able to identify with both as an expression of our time and as an attempt to continue urban culture, we will have to create a durable architecture which is able to grow a patina and which is not always under pressure to be new. I am in no way trying to say that our buildings should be as solid as those built a hundred years ago. That is no longer possible. Nor do I want to unleash a new discussion of style. But I do believe that we quite rightly yearn for a "stone" architecture which stands firmly on the ground, is firmly anchored and is permanent, not just passing by. Aldo Rossi spoke about permanence as being essential if buildings are to be an expression of our collective memory. That is what I am talking about here.[1]

[1] Hans Kollhoff, "High-Rise Buildings" [1993], trans. Chris Charlesworth, in *Kollhoff: Examples*, by Annegret Burg (Basel: Birkhäuser, 1998), 195. Originally published as Hans Kollhoff, "Städtebaulicher Ideenwettbewerb Alexanderplatz," in *Asphalt und Licht oder: Hinter der Weltstadt*, ed. Cornelius Hertling and Nicolette Baumeister (Berlin: Architektenkammer, 1994), 30–31.

above Eunil Cho, pin up, Berlin

Introduction

This book is the product of an advanced graduate design studio taught by Hans Kollhoff with Kyle Dugdale at Yale School of Architecture. Broadly stated, the studio addressed the role of the skyscraper in the contemporary city, taking as point of departure Hans Kollhoff's own master plan for Berlin's Alexanderplatz. The studio's lessons, however, extended far beyond the context of Berlin. Its more pointed contention was to insist that the tower bears a public responsibility that in turn places certain demands upon the architect. Those demands must inform decisions about material, tectonic, and scale, just as they must take account of climate, cost, and collective memory. But above all, the tower's design must embody a serious commitment to the public space of the city.

The book opens with the studio brief, describing specific challenges and laying out terms of engagement. This is followed by a collection of prompts that draw on Hans Kollhoff's body of written work to offer a taste of the studio's characteristic dialogue, leading to a presentation of the carefully worded exercises that shaped the studio's process. Two essays by Hans Kollhoff and by Kyle Dugdale offer provocations that illuminate particular aspects of the studio's concerns: one illustrating the power of the idea of the tectonic within the trajectory of architecture's history, the other based upon close observation of the contemporary city. The book then presents, in texts and images, each of the eleven projects designed by the students, before closing with an acknowledgment of its various participants.

Some readers may find this book to be out of step with the discipline's current preoccupations. It is our hope that a closer examination of its contents will show this to be not a weakness but a strength.

Contexts

Berlin's Alexanderplatz is a large and culturally significant open space at the historic city center's eastern periphery. Host to the nightlife of 1920s Weimar Germany, an architectural showpiece for postwar East German socialism, and the site of ongoing political demonstrations, it has been subject to intense scrutiny since Berlin's designation as the capital of a reunified Germany. The area remains at the center of public debate about redevelopment within the city.

Our urban design for this area is composed of a figural public open square defined by the surrounding city blocks. These blocks act as pedestals that are in turn articulated by an array of towers that rise from the rear of each block. The plan has undergone a process of functional and spatial adaptation to contemporary requirements, and a number of adjacent buildings, significant to the history of East German urban development, have been designated for historic preservation.

Contentions

The European skyscraper is not simply an extrusion of the site, driven by property value, but rather a vertical extension of the earth. At the heart of this studio is the contention that the European high-rise tower is imbued with public responsibility, competing with the towers of churches and city halls, together with which it dominates the city's physiognomy both physically and symbolically. *Property demands commitment.*

The heroes of modern architecture—from Le Corbusier and Mies van der Rohe to Louis Kahn—understood architecture to be an extrusion of the earth rather than a constructed artifact to be dropped onto the ground plane. Architecture was consequently interpreted as a monolithic whole, even if assembled from parts. The highly ambiguous phenomenon of visual entities seen in relation to bodily existence, simultaneously nothing but a compilation of heterogeneous events, was called *Tektonik*. I prefer the singular *tectonic* to the plural *tectonics*, which obscures the precise and fundamental role that the term plays in architecture. *Without tectonic there is no architecture.*

Tectonic treatment is the articulation of mass by means of *lineamento*, profiling, which accomplishes both the separation and the unification of the elements from which architecture is composed. Articulated mass as monolithic extrusion of the earth, articulated in relation to our visual sensibility, which is in fact bodily—that is what I call architecture.

Tasks

Our studio tested the feasibility of the modified urban plan for Alexanderplatz, understanding this process as a case study with potential for broader application elsewhere. The task was to design

Towers in the City

Studio Brief, Hans Kollhoff

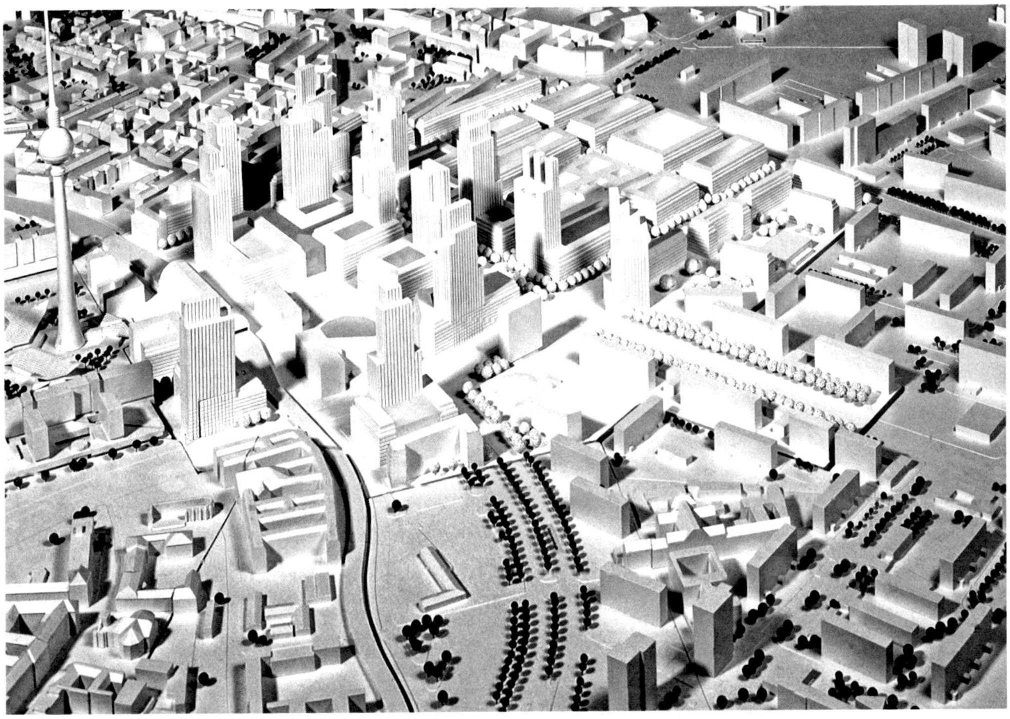

eleven multifunctional urban blocks with towers, each limited to a height of 150 meters. We analyzed the urban context and developed individual architectural projects. We started our design process by making clay *bozzetti* according to the rules of the land use plan, in a manner comparable to that in which Hugh Ferriss interpreted New York City's setback regulations in the 1920s, turning them into breathtaking expressionist buildings and spaces.

above Hans Kollhoff and Helga Timmermann, Alexanderplatz master plan site model, 1993

The projects were developed in plan, section, and elevation, with corresponding analysis of significant interior perspectives. We worked toward large-scale models to test the projects' potential to establish an exceptional public space within the best tradition of European urbanism, offering a contribution to the ongoing public debate in Germany's capital city.

Prompts

above Students' models for *Bozzetto* exercise. The exercise prompt notes that the block "is intended to be a stable base from which the tower projects upward." Tower, *n.* definition 1: "A building lofty in proportion to the size of its base."

Tower and City

From the *Oxford English Dictionary*, abbr.[1]

tower, *n.*

1. A building lofty in proportion to the size of its base, either isolated, or forming part of a castle, church, or other edifice, or of the walls of a town.
2. a. Such a structure used as a stronghold.
   b. In early religious use, often applied to heaven.
3. *figurative*. Frequently in *tower of strength*. See also ivory tower *n.*
4. *transferred.* A lofty pile or material mass.
5. b. The 'castle' borne on the back of an elephant. *Obsolete.*
6. Applied to various things having the form, figure, or appearance of a tower.
   a. *Chess.* The Castle or Rook. *Obsolete.*
   b. A very high head-dress worn by women in the reigns of William III and Anne. It was built up in the form of a tower of pasteboard, muslin, lace, and ribbons. *Historical.*

city, *n.*

1. A town or other inhabited place. *Obsolete.*
2. a. A municipality traditionally or officially designated a city, being larger in size or population, or having greater status, than a town.
   c. The built-up and densely inhabited part of a region as distinguished from the countryside.
3. a. The inhabitants of a city considered collectively.
   b. The official or legal representatives of the inhabitants of a city; the city authorities.
4. In extended use and *figurative*.
   a. In religious language: heaven or paradise, portrayed as a city. Frequently in *celestial city*, *heavenly city*, etc.
5. *Ancient History*. A Greek or Roman city-state; = polis *n.*

[1] For full entries see *Oxford English Dictionary*, s.v. "tower, n.1" and "city, n.," https://www.oed.com.

The European City

Hans Kollhoff

What I am concerned with is the social significance of memory as manifested in buildings—the vessels which relativize the storms of the moment—in which the moment is in a sense safely preserved. Without these vessels, the moment is all there is, everything appears for a brief moment only to be swept away in the current of time without any hope of being anchored in history. The moment and nothingness: that is the fate of the young mega-cities of Asia and South America, for which the European city has long ceased to be a useful model, and not simply because urban civilisation can only begin when poverty is at an end. The European city is captured time, moments that have been caught using the means available to architecture. . . . It is not a question of new versus old, but of continuity.[1]

[1] Hans Kollhoff, "The European City" [1993], trans. Chris Charlesworth, in *Kollhoff: Examples*, by Annegret Burg (Basel: Birkhäuser, 1998), 190. Abridged version originally published in *Das Schloss? Eine Ausstellung über die Mitte Berlins*, 2nd ed. (Berlin: Wilhelm Ernst und Sohn, 1993), 120–21.

image Alexanderstraße, Berlin

above Senate Department for Urban Development and Housing, Berlin, 1:1000 scale model
opposite Rudolph Hall, New Haven, blackboard after an afternoon of studio instruction

Urban Fabric

Hans Kollhoff

We will have to take note of the fact that the urban fabric is seldom the result of one great architectural stroke, seldom a one-off creation—and that successful urban structure is only in exceptional cases, for a particular purpose at a particular place, dependent on great architecture.[1]

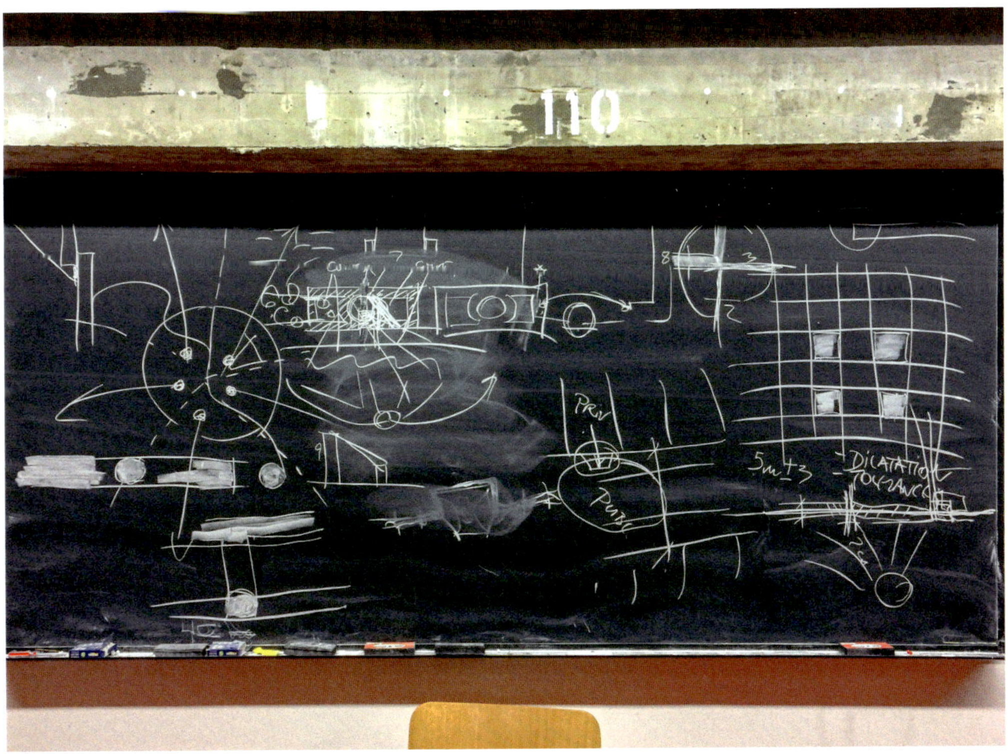

[1] Hans Kollhoff, "Schlosspalast, Haus und Stadt" [1993], trans. Chris Charlesworth, in *Kollhoff: Examples*, by Annegret Burg (Basel: Birkhäuser, 1998), 183. Abridged version originally published in *Das Schloss? Eine Ausstellung über die Mitte Berlins*, 2nd ed. (Berlin: Wilhelm Ernst und Sohn, 1993), 120–21.

above Photographs of Berlin, February 14–19, 2016

You can't love or hate Berlin,

above Photographs of Berlin, February 14–19, 2016

you have to do both at once.[1]

[1] Hans Kollhoff, "La Berlino di Hans Kollhoff, Hans Kollhoff's Berlin," *Domus* 996 (November 2015): 119.

Structural Principles

Hans Kollhoff

Structural principles cannot be invented, only discovered.[1]

[1] Hans Kollhoff, "Schlosspalast, Haus und Stadt" [1993], trans. Chris Charlesworth, in *Kollhoff: Examples*, by Annegret Burg (Basel: Birkhäuser, 1998), 185. Abridged version originally published in *Das Schloss? Eine Ausstellung über die Mitte Berlins*, 2nd ed. (Berlin: Wilhelm Ernst und Sohn, 1993), 120–21.

left Gustav Erdmann, cemetery chapel, Georgenfriedhof, Berlin, 1867

From time immemorial, architecture has been the art of making it possible to forget the inadequacies of the building process. The careful layering of less or more precisely dressed stones was superseded by the aesthetic attraction of masonry bonds. The image of the jointed wall promises the eye stability, security, safety—quite independent of the actual structural system, provided that the image is not unmasked at some decisive point as post-Modern wallpaper. Today we no longer build with thick blocks of stone. We use stones in slabs of 3 to 6 centimetres thickness, depending on the dimensions and hardness of the stone.

The arrangement of the slabs on the façade can follow two opposing principles. The building can be treated as an abstract cube onto which a rectangular grid is superimposed and which is then divided up into manageable sections. This is the procedure most commonly used today, as it claims to "honestly" express the structure. That is why unpointed joints are allowed to be seen and glimpses of stainless steel anchors bear witness to late-Functionalist consciousness. Slight doubts begin to appear, however, when it comes to the untidy image of joints with assembly tolerances of between 5 and 11 millimetres, and it becomes positively precarious when economy is elevated to the sole architectural principle. . . . When the difference between pavement and façade can barely be distinguished, the desire for abstraction has surely gone too far even for dyed-in-the-wool Modernists.

The alternative is to treat the building as an object: the slabs are joined according to tectonic principles which acknowledge the fact that buildings have a top and bottom, that the roof termination has to fulfil different expectations from the ground line and that the window sill is not the same as the lintel. If you follow tectonic principles, possibilities for a building to express itself re-emerge from oblivion, possibilities which go beyond simply expressing the theme of loads and bearing but which also relate things once more to the human body.[1]

[1] Hans Kollhoff, "Tectonics and Façade" [1997], trans. Chris Charlesworth, in *Kollhoff: Examples*, by Annegret Burg (Basel: Birkhäuser, 1998), 190–91. Originally published as "Hofgarten am Gendarmenmarket, Friedrichstraße 79," *Bauwelt*, February 14, 1997, 300.

Tectonics and Façade

Hans Kollhoff

above and left Reconstruction mockup of Schinkel's Bauakademie, Schinkelplatz, Berlin—partially built in brick masonry and partially hand-painted on vinyl (folded at left). The didactic masterpiece of an architect whose career began with painted stage sets and ended with solid masonry, Schinkel's Bauakademie stands in a lineage of rational structures that leads toward the early skyscrapers of New York and Chicago.

I still remember frost patterns on the windows in winter. Those days are over and I sometimes see that as a loss.

We are reminded in this connection of a discussion between Auguste Perret and Le Corbusier about the nature of the window. Is the window an abstract strip which provides a panorama, as Le Corbusier believed, or is it an element, the proportions of which have to adapt to the human body, as Auguste Perret saw it? For him, the window was a vertical element with two leaves which a person standing could open with a characteristic movement and then stand in the opening and possibly lean out.[1]

[1] Hans Kollhoff, "Windows" [1995], trans. Chris Charlesworth, in *Kollhoff: Examples*, by Annegret Burg (Basel: Birkhäuser, 1998), 196. Originally published as "Metrik und Tektonik," in *Fenster: Architektur und Technologie im Dialog*, ed. Günther Uhlig, Niklaus Kohler, and Lothar Schneider (Braunschweig: Vieweg, 1994), 66–74.

Windows

Hans Kollhoff

left Ludwig Mies van der Rohe, Perls House, Berlin-Zehlendorf, 1911
above Platoon Cultural Development, Kunsthalle, Berlin-Mitte, 2012

La modénature est la pierre de touche de l'architecte.[1]

Die Profilierung ist der Prüfstein des Architekten.[2]

Contour and profile are the touchstone of the architect.[3]

[1] Le Corbusier, *Vers une architecture* (Paris: Éditions Crès, 1923), x.

[2] Le Corbusier, *Kommende Baukunst*, trans. Hans Hildebrandt (Stuttgart, Berlin, and Leipzig: Deutsche Verlags-Anstalt, 1926), xiv.

[3] Le Corbusier, *Towards a New Architecture*, trans. Frederick Etchells (London: John Rodker, 1927), 5–6.

Contour and Profile

Le Corbusier

above, left to right Contour and profile details, Berlin: Hans Henselmann, Frankfurter Tor, Karl-Marx-Allee, 1953–57; Rykestraße 51, Prenzlauer Berg; Karl Friedrich Schinkel, Schlossbrücke, Unter den Linden, 1821–24

[1] Hans Kollhoff, "The Industrialisation of Building" [1994], trans. Chris Charlesworth, in *Kollhoff: Examples*, by Annegret Burg (Basel: Birkhäuser, 1998), 192–93. Originally published in *Deutsches Architektur-Museum Architektur Jahrbuch* (1994): 9–10.

image Manfred Hörner, Peter Senf, and Joachim Härter, Haus der Statistik, Otto-Braun-Straße, Berlin, 1970

Wear and Tear

Hans Kollhoff

The industrialisation of building, a mantra of modern architecture and perhaps its most radical vision, has evidently been thoroughly sounded out now. . . . Everything has been tried, and the balance sheet is sobering. Even those examples that have been classified as revolutionary are now in a pitiful state; many have been demolished. That has its own rationale, since quite a few of the projects which were built using industrialised manufacturing methods had a provisional character—buildings are no longer designed to last for all eternity, it is said, buildings are subject to wear and tear just as a car is. After a number of years they will be demolished and replaced by more modern ones.

Nevertheless, we have now moved away from this naive idolization of progress: sensitised to ecological and economic considerations, we are critical of the products of our affluent consumer society. What began with such promise—the idea of building participating in the blessings of mass production—is now mercilessly striking back.[1]

The High-Rise

Hans Kollhoff

Recalling the early American skyscrapers, along the street, after a while, you don't look at the tops anymore, and the street functions like any European street. On the street level, you need a base, entrances, and storefronts, so building height is not so important. I learned from New York and Chicago that, above a certain height, you don't need to indicate the roofline. In Chicago, Sullivan started to neglect the roofline. Entrepreneurs and architects became much more interested in the idea of verticality, so they pulled the building into the sky. . . .

There's a lot to do today to bring architecture back to the ground again. . . .

Look at Hugh Ferriss's renderings, which feel as if the buildings are created from the earth, from the urban texture, and pulled toward the sky—in the same way Le Corbusier's sketches of the Acropolis make it look as if it were an extrusion of the earth.[1]

[1] Hans Kollhoff in conversation with Nina Rappaport, *Constructs* 18, no. 2 (Spring 2016): 5.

The studio visited New York City, paying particular attention to urban texture, and comparing the city's early skyscrapers to Ludwig Mies van der Rohe's postwar Seagram Building and to more recent work by Robert A. M. Stern and by Frank Gehry.

opposite Raymond Hood / Associated Architects, 30 Rockefeller Plaza, New York City, 1933
above left Raymond Hood / Associated Architects, 50 Rockefeller Plaza, New York City, 1932: base detail at entrance, with shot sawed limestone cladding, granite base, bluestone paving, and bronze corner reinforcement
above right Frank Gehry, 8 Spruce Street, New York City, 2011

above Alfred Messel, Volks-Kaffee- und Speise-Hallen-Gesellschaft, Neue Schönhauser Straße 13, Berlin-Kreuzberg, 1890–91

A market that is designed for mass consumption

knows very well how to create a need for the most ridiculous "innovations" and makes the cynical comment that democracy is when everyone can have whatever they desire. As long as a consensus existed about how people should live together in society—and in particular in an urban setting—and as long as there was a corresponding convention about architecture, modern life, no matter how future-oriented it might be, was contained within the vessel of the historical place. In those days, life today was lived against the background of yesterday, which was present, visible and understandable for everyone: within the walls of the houses of the city. The city was the product of generations of effort.[1]

[1] Hans Kollhoff, "Schlosspalast, Haus und Stadt" [1993], trans. Chris Charlesworth, in *Kollhoff: Examples*, by Annegret Burg (Basel: Birkhäuser, 1998), 188. Abridged version originally published in *Das Schloss? Eine Ausstellung über die Mitte Berlins*, 2nd ed. (Berlin: Wilhelm Ernst und Sohn, 1993), 120–21.

Process

above Clay models prepared for Assignment 1: Bozzetto

Assignments

Hans Kollhoff

How will we proceed?

We will start with rather playful exercises, and step by step in a cumulative design process we will arrive at a professionally drafted project which we will visualize in realistic renderings and large-scale models. Every step will be discussed individually.

Assignment 1: Bozzetto
Assignment 2: Living Room
Assignment 3: Front, Entrance
Assignment 4: Plan, Elevation, Perspective
Assignment 5: Light, Shadow, Mass
Assignment 6: Site, Core
Assignment 7: Tectonic

Model in clay, with your hands, at least six alternatives for the block-tower configuration. Each must be perceived clearly as a volumetric entity or, more precisely, as a bodily whole. The block is intended to be a stable base from which the tower projects upward, terminating—thanks to its setbacks—almost weightlessly toward the sky. Concentrate on the dynamics of the contour in order to avoid an additive character.

Quick intuitive modeling of many alternatives rather than developing geometrical options in advance will lead more easily to successful results. Proceed by trial and error—modeling, destroying, remodeling—until you have at least six alternatives that are of equal morphological significance. The ground plane should be approximately 8 x 8 cm, the height 15 cm.

Finally, name the alternatives as precisely as possible with one term.

Bozzetto

Assignment 1

Design, in perspective, three living rooms in three categories—studio, market-rate one-bedroom, and luxury apartment—each with a view over the city. Pay attention to the relationship between glass and wall surface, since the building should read as a solid stone structure. Of equal importance is the related exterior space: balcony, wintergarden, loggia, or terrace.

Draw three perspectives with corresponding living room plans and corresponding exterior elevations, at a scale of 1:50. The interior perspective should in each instance be a rendering, by hand or on computer, in color; eye level should be in a sitting position, at 1.20 or 1.30 m. The apartments should be furnished.

right Richard Green, studies for exterior elevations and interior perspectives

Living Room

Assignment 2

Design the plan of the entrance sequence to your tower within the given location at a scale of 1:200. You do not have to design the entire ground floor plan. Draw the tower front at 1:200 scale on the basis of the façade treatment of your previous exercise. Pay attention to the relief as a reflection of both functional conditions (balconies, bay windows, terraces, loggias, roof gardens etc.) and structural conditions (pilasters, cornices etc.) by constructing the shadow precisely.

above Kollhoff Architekten, Reinhardtstraße 33, Berlin

Front, Entrance

Assignment 3

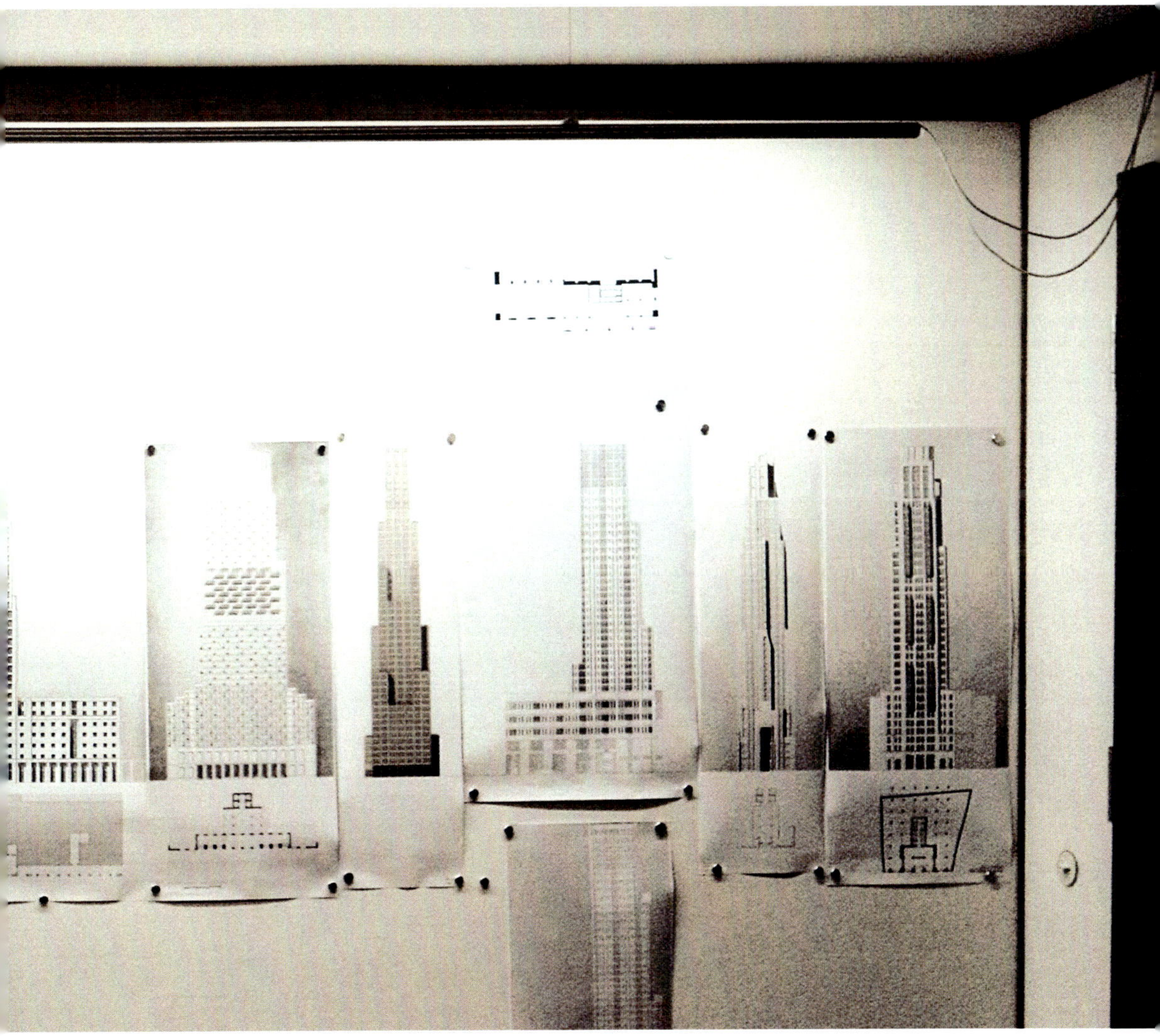

Design three tower plans—at lower, intermediate and upper residential levels—in order to draw a revised front elevation and a corresponding side elevation, at a scale of 1:200. Show the corner in perspective (with constructed shadows) seen from pedestrian eye level.

right Dov Feinmesser, corner perspective study

Plan, Elevation, Perspective

Assignment 4

Translate the corner perspective of the previous exercise into a charcoal drawing that emphasizes the mass of the building by concentrating on light and shadow. The height of the paper should be precisely 1.7 m. Follow Hugh Ferriss's sequential drawing technique.

Proper Charcoal Drawing Method

1. Compressed charcoal only. Vine charcoal banned.
2. Basement drawing studio only.
3. Use far end of drawing studio to increase distance to carpet.
4. Protect surface around drawing, protect flooring under drawing, protect everything.
5. Dispose daintily of protection when done.
6. Check shoes and hands before leaving drawing studio.
7. Fix charcoal before transporting through Rudolph Hall.
8. But do not use fixative in the building.
9. You are being assessed, and charcoal privileges may be revoked for irresponsible drawing.
10. Keep your dirty hands off the white folding chairs in the drawing studio.
11. As there are no disposable shoe covers available for sale in downtown New Haven, use a pair of socks to similar effect.
12. Remove said socks upon exiting drawing studio.
13. Drawing studio is available all day Saturday, all day Sunday, Monday morning, all day Tuesday, Wednesday morning.[1]

[1] Kyle Dugdale, email to studio after extensive negotiations with Rudolph Hall administrative and custodial staff, March 3, 2016.

Light, Shadow, Mass

Assignment 5

above @YSOAofficial: "Students in Hans Kollhoff's studio (designing buildings for Berlin's Alexanderplatz) are caught in the act of actually drawing, by hand, massive charcoal renderings for their mid-review presentations"—receiving more *likes* than any prior image in the history of the school's Facebook page.
https://www.facebook.com/YSOAofficial/photos/

Insert your building into the Alexanderplatz site plan. Indicate entrance, roof, terraces, etc. at a scale of 1:500. Concentrate on the core-configuration of your building in plan (ground, intermediate, top) and section, at a scale of 1:200. Pay attention to the spatial quality of the lobbies. Draw the main entrance in a perspective rendering that shows materiality, color, furniture, light, etc.

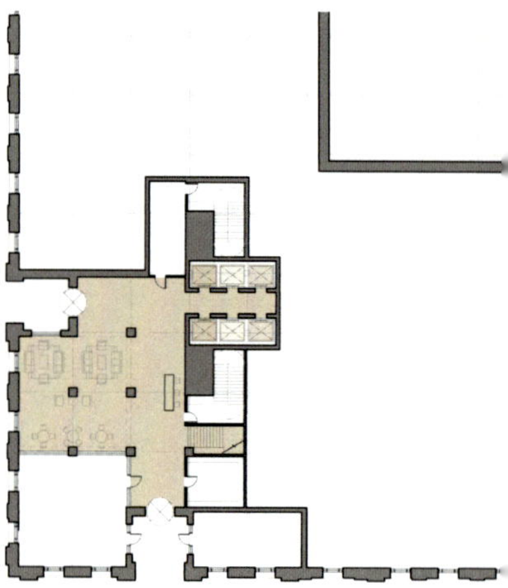

above Gina Cannistra, study for entrance lobby and core

Site, Core

Assignment 6

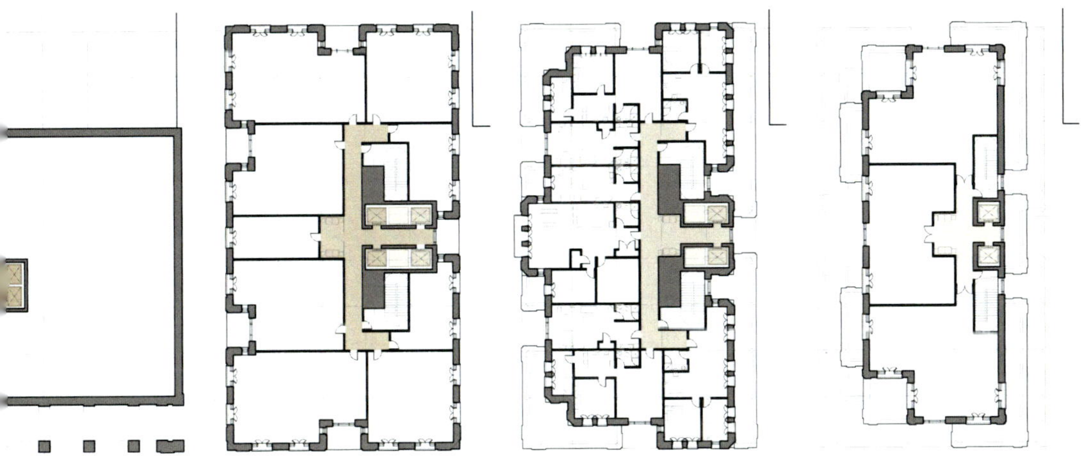

Show the construction of the typical corner condition of an upper floor (including terrace/balcony) in plan, section, and elevation, at scales of 1:20, 1:10, 1:5, and 1:1.

Concentrate on the tectonic treatment of critical conditions (base/shop front, colonnade, cornice/lintel/corner, crown, etc.) in alternative three-dimensional freehand sketches. Choose at least three different conditions and develop at least three possible sketch alternatives for each situation. Look at Schinkel's Schauspielhaus and at the twenty volumes of MoMA's Mies van der Rohe Archive series.

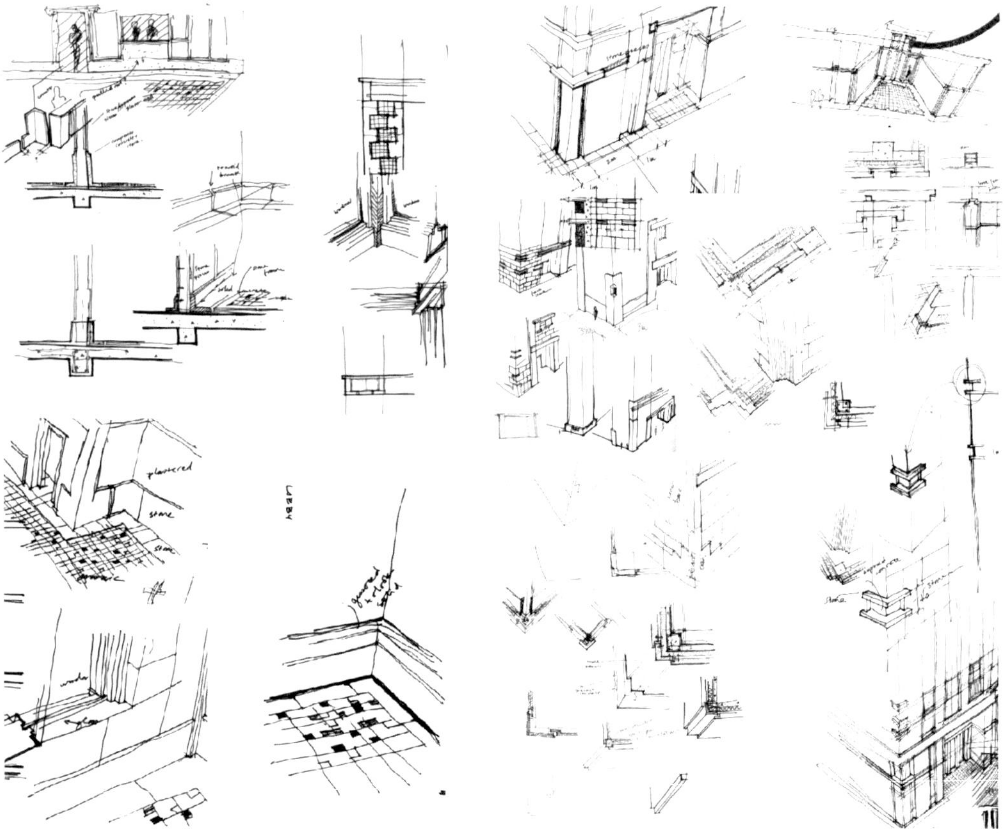

above Aymar Mariño-Maza, corner condition study sketches

Tectonic

Assignment 7

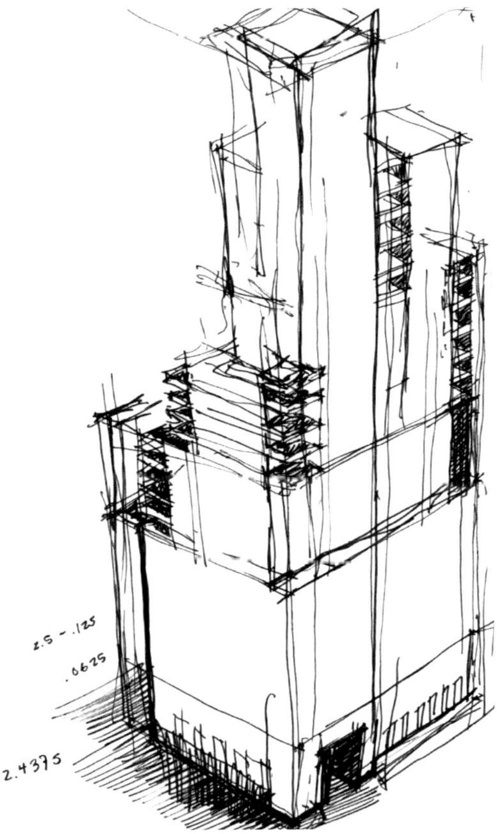

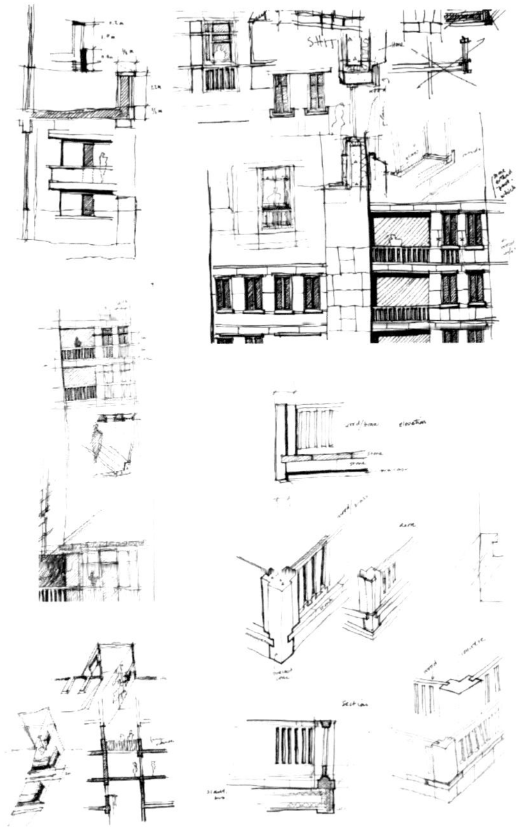

Provocations

above Friedrich Gilly, Perspective Study, 1798/99
Staatliche Museen zu Berlin, Kunstbibliothek, photograph Dietmar Katz, public domain

Return of the Tectonic

Hans Kollhoff

On his first journey to Italy in 1803–1805, Karl Friedrich Schinkel passed rather quickly through Venice, Florence, and Rome, and headed instead for southern Italy. He was already intimately familiar with the treatises of Palladio. But the reception of Greek and Roman antiquity by the architects of the Renaissance was, for him, evidently too quick, and perhaps superficial. He wanted instead to begin prior to Rome, and to leave the Baroque behind. The Baroque could already be felt in the work of Palladio, and what he himself needed to overcome back in Berlin was, precisely, the Baroque.

He knew how difficult that would be. The challenge was to strip architecture in order to rehabilitate tectonics, and it seemed more promising to begin with the naked cube. So in southern Italy he sought out the architecture of the Greeks—not their temples, but their vernacular houses. And from this journey he took home the practices that would distinguish him from the architects of the Renaissance: the domestic scale employed even for monumental buildings, the rigor of compact volumes, and the emphasis on refined tectonic articulation. Here he succeeded in developing building as a civil art: the accomplishment that would later impress Adolf Loos.

The farmhouses of Sicily are simple volumes set within hilly landscapes, growing from the earth—their steps, stairs and terraces decidedly part of the earth, stabilized only by verticals and horizontals, sometimes completed by the oblique lines of roofs and railings. There is nothing superfluous to spoil the impression of sculpted earth, and one is reminded of the wonderful drawing by Friedrich Gilly, intended for the purpose of teaching perspective drawing, but ultimately a manifesto: cubic volumes in the sand.

In order to become architecture, these cubes must be opened without losing their unity and serenity. The role of the architect is not that of the engineer or of the artist, of the professional or of the specialist in sophisticated tastes, and it is certainly not that of the connoisseur of styles. Instead, the architect is obliged to confront the straightforward questions of the common man.

The task of the art of building, argues Schinkel, is to make life visible. As he observes in the annotations to one of his most provocative sheets of sketches, now in Berlin,

> Nota bene:
>
> In order to gain results what is required is not long-winded philosophical argument, but rather pure intuition based on direct observation.
>
> Architectural relationships are based on the common laws of physics, but ultimately become truly meaningful only through reference and analogy to the individual's existence as a human being.[1]

Text translated from *Q.E.D.* (Cologne: Walther König, forthcoming).

[1] Karl Friedrich Schinkel, "Die architectonischen Verhältnisse," ca. 1828, Schinkel Archive 4.79.40, Zentralarchiv, Staatliche Museen zu Berlin, my translation. For a transcription of the German text see Karl Friedrich Schinkel, *Das Architektonische Lehrbuch*, ed. Goerd Peschken (Berlin: Deutscher Kunstverlag, 2001), 45.

113 Stets weitläufige philosophische Begründung soll hier der reinen Gestalt bei unmittelbarer Anschauung in Anspruch genommen werden, um Resultate zu erhalten.

Die architektonischen Verhältnisse beruhen auf ganz allgemeinen statischen Gesetzen, werden aber erst recht bedeutend durch Beziehung und Analogie der persönlichen Existenz des Menschen zunächst und der ihm ähnlich gebildeten u. organisirten Wesen der Natur. [illegible] immer die statischen Gesetze, mechanischen Gesetze zum Grunde liegen, [illegible] die Individuen [illegible] Bewegung [illegible] ausgedrückt, [illegible] Achsen- und Mittel-Gesetze befindet. [illegible] Fig A [illegible] mit der [illegible] Sicherheit überzeugt [illegible], indem er [illegible] die beiden Öffnungen [illegible] Massen [illegible] durch die Mitte der Pfeiler zwischen denselben [illegible], wie über u. unter den Öffnungen volle Masse zum Zusammenhalten vorhanden ist.

— Wie wird bei Fig B nicht das Gefühl der [illegible] erregt, indem der kleine Pfeilerchen durch Überwölbung u. der großen Masse die darauf liegt viel zu [illegible] ist, und diese Construction unmöglich [illegible] wenn nicht die große Mauermasse zur Seite der Öffnungen [illegible].

— Wer fühlt nicht, daß Fig C den Charakter der Leichtigkeit hat, indem die leeren Räume der Öffnungen im Verhältniß der Massen [illegible] und überwiegend sind, die Massen [illegible] auf die Pfeiler vertheilt zu dieser [illegible] und die Ganze der Stütze [illegible] gesichert erscheint.

— Wer [illegible] nicht bei Fig. D. den [illegible] der Bögen, [illegible] mit [illegible] der Schwere-Gesetze die Masse durch die [illegible] [illegible] [illegible] über die großen Öffnungen [illegible] diese Bewegung in der Form [illegible] [illegible] in der Form [illegible] daß [illegible] Massen [illegible] Richtung d' [illegible] Richtung [illegible] entgegengesetzten und [illegible] Gleichgewicht [illegible].

— Weshalb wird bei Fig E die [illegible] einer [illegible] und sichern Massen-Vertheilung [illegible] befriedigend gefühlt wird, wo die [illegible] Quadratischen Form E'E'E'E' [illegible] die gewöhnlichen Halbkreisform E'E''E' [illegible] [illegible] [illegible] Weite [illegible] füllen läßt. Wo die [illegible] [illegible] Massen [illegible] gesichert sind, daß das [illegible] E'E''E'''E⁴ [illegible] doppelt [illegible] E'E'''E⁵E⁶ [illegible] Wiederholt [illegible] Fülle.

— Wer fühlt in F nicht das [illegible] der Massen-Verhältnisse [illegible] mechanischen [illegible] und [illegible] Verankerung in F'F'' nöthig wird.

— Fig G [illegible] [illegible] sein [illegible] durch findet [illegible] [illegible] [illegible] [illegible] [illegible] Construction bringen wollte, daß [illegible] diese Art der [illegible] auf der [illegible] [illegible] (diese [illegible]) [illegible] den Capitellstücke [illegible] Säule [illegible] die [illegible] Art [illegible] Wirkung als die der vollkommenste [illegible] zeigt.

— Fig H die [illegible] Ruhe [illegible] [illegible] und die [illegible] Schwere-Gesetze in [illegible] wirksam.

— Fig I [illegible] [illegible] Charakter der Schwere [illegible].

— Fig K [illegible] den Charakter der [illegible] [illegible], Ruhe, Feinheit, Verhältniß [illegible]

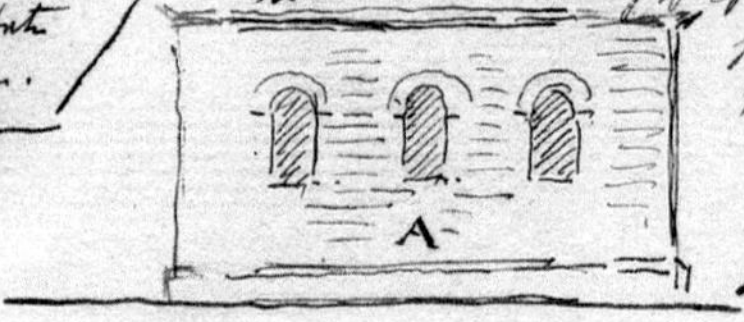

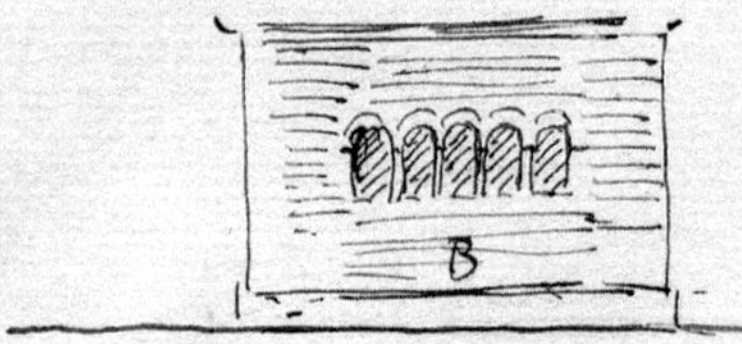

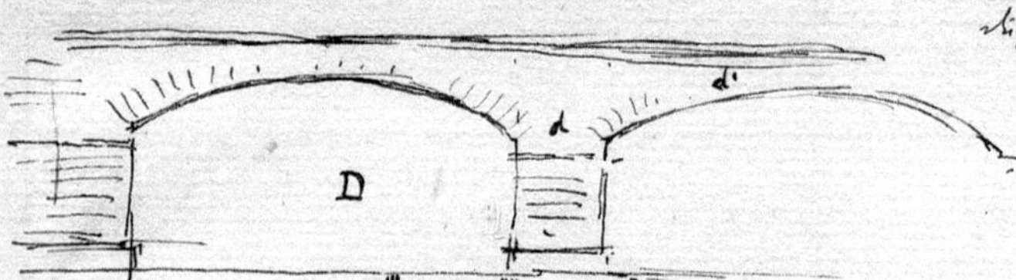

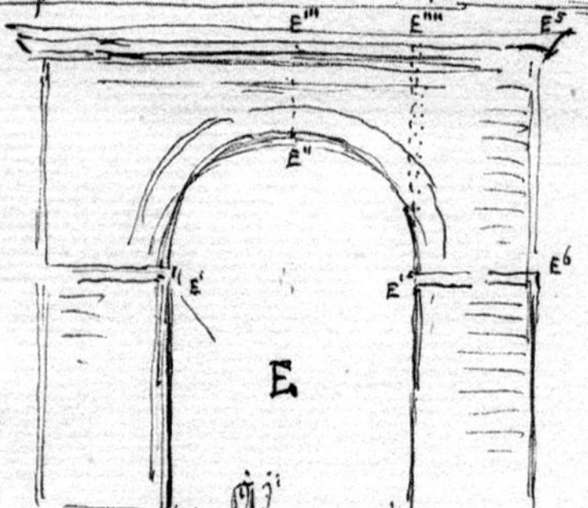

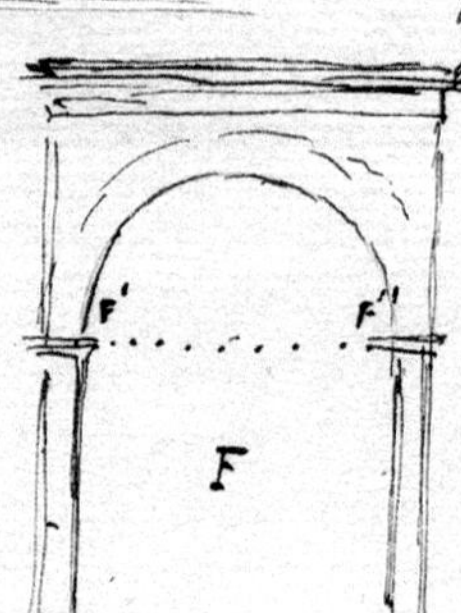

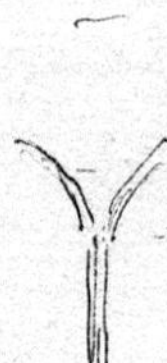

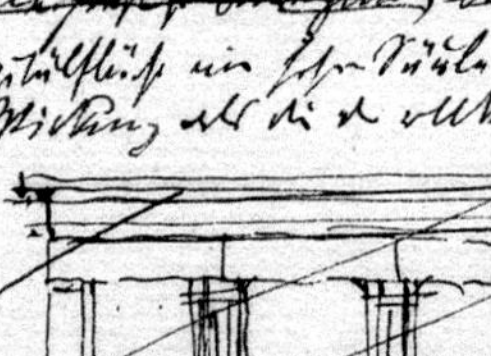

In lieu of extracting answers from Renaissance treatises, the architect must confront a series of rhetorical questions. For example:

> In figure A, who would not be convinced of the sense of security established by the relationships between parts, seeing how the openings of the building gain a quiet stability through the strength of the pillars that stand between them, with solid mass providing cohesion above and below those openings?
>
> Who would not feel the sense of riskiness in figure B, the tiny columns overtasked by the heavy mass that lies above the vaulting, such that this structure would be impossible without the massive walls adjacent to the openings?
>
> Who would not feel that figure C has a character of lightness, with the empty spaces of the openings possessing importance and dominance in relation to the mass? The weight of the entablature and vaulting is equally distributed among the columns, in relation to which it does not seem too heavy, since the whole is secured by stronger corner pillars.
>
> In figure D, who would not gain the impression of daring, as if the laws of gravity were being disregarded? By an artificially created lateral pressure the mass almost jumps across the large openings, and yet this movement has to be considered as fixed, gaining safety and composure of form through the existence of sufficiently strong masses and through equal counterbalancing forces that accomplish equilibrium.
>
> Who does not, in figure E, gain the impression of a distribution of mass that is grand and secure, devoid of any pressure, where the spaciousness of the square form E'E'E'E', enlarged by the comfortable half-circle E'E''E', makes it feel both high and wide? The masses enclosing this space are firmly secured, with the small floating piece E'E''E'''E'''' given sufficient hold by its attachment both to the element E'E''''E^5E^6, which is twice as big, and to the other half of the work.
>
> Who does not, in figure F, see a precarious proportioning of mass, setting in motion mechanical processes that require artificial anchoring at F'F''?
>
> Figure G, tall and light, maintains its standing through equal and opposite forces that hold one another up, wishing to make their equality visible by performing this supporting act—this antagonism—on the refined uppermost surface of the capital of a tall column, which registers no effect other than that of absolute repose.
>
> Figure H, the highest tranquility drawn out by building, the simplest laws of gravity working upon large masses.
>
> Figure I likewise, emerging from the very character of weight.
>
> Figure K, which attains the character of beauty, of stillness, freedom, balance.[2]

The issue here has nothing to do with style, and there are no recipes of the sort that we know from architectural treatises. Instead architecture presents itself as tectonic matter of fact, the human being face to face with the artefact upon the earth. Schinkel spends a conspicuously long time, while still at the beginning of his journey, repeatedly sketching the grottos between the cliffs of the karst. He produces line drawings that remind one of Morandi, looking out to sea, the motif of romanticism and the fundamental tectonic condition par excellence: the horizon and, standing upright, the human being.

What was once called "tectonic" began to dissolve toward the end of the eighteenth century, during a crisis of symmetry provoked by the English

left Karl Friedrich Schinkel, Architectonic Relationships, ca. 1828 Staatliche Museen zu Berlin, Zentralarchiv, Nachlass Karl Friedrich Schinkel, SMB-ZA, IV/NL Schinkel 79, Bl. 40, used by permission

[2] Karl Friedrich Schinkel, Architektonischen Verhältnisse, ca. 1828, Staatliche Museen zu Berlin, Zentralarchiv, Nachlass Karl Friedrich Schinkel, SMB-ZA, IV/NL Schinkel 79, Bl. 40, my translation. Figure references are keyed to drawings as reproduced at left.

top Karl Friedrich Schinkel, Farmhouse, Capri, 1804
Staatliche Museen zu Berlin, Kupferstichkabinett, SM 5.31, Creative Commons BY-NC-SA

above Karl Friedrich Schinkel, Coastline at Castelvetrano, Sicily, 1804
Staatliche Museen zu Berlin, Kupferstichkabinett, SM 6b.59, Creative Commons BY-NC-SA

landscape garden and its "picturesque" ideal—which did not come to a stop when it encountered architecture.

Schinkel longed for freedom from the straight-jacket of the orders and treatises, for a return to a cubic architecture. In the landscape beyond the city gates he discovered an architectonic dialogue with topography and the horizon—a sentiment that Le Corbusier would recall a century later in his sketches of the Acropolis.

When the term "architectural composition" replaced the "tectonic" in the mid-nineteenth century, interest shifted from content to effect. The floodgates were opened to the confusion that ultimately led to the early twentieth century's hopeless debate over form and function—a debate that is not over yet. So we may benefit from recalling the significance of "tectonic," a term in which the antagonistic spheres are both contained in their ongoing dialogue. Through the "tectonic" and its ambiguous nature it should be possible to overcome the fruitless debate that has paralyzed the past century.

The 1904 edition of the volume on "Architectonic Composition" in the monumental *Handbuch der Architektur* (*Handbook of Architecture*) still insists that "to design a building one must be master of construction as well as master of form."[3] But in the 1926 edition, under the headline "Building as Art," Fritz Schumacher speaks only of building design (*Gestalten*). Even "architectonic composition" is no longer mentioned, notwithstanding its survival in the book's title. What remains is August Thiersch's doctrine of proportion, which also deals with the Erechtheion, "that peculiar example of an asymmetrical but still harmoniously arranged ensemble of buildings."[4] The Erechtheion, a link between temple and country house: unfortunately Schinkel never saw it with his own eyes.

Even in the "work- and form-course" (*Werk- und Formlehre*) of Walter Gropius's Bauhaus this unity was still implied by the "and"—although the focus was now on "artistic design, predominantly for building."[5] Soon after, building was confronted with avant-gardist concepts of art that led to the disappearance of architecture, subsumed within product design. The picturesque as it infected our profession from Poussin to Kandinsky here demonstrates its devastating effect, where "form" ultimately serves only as a means to add interest to the functional diagram. "Make things interesting," suggested Gropius to his students—thereby proving that the legend of the path of progress from Schinkel to the Bauhaus is a misunderstanding, if not a fantasy.

[3] Heinrich Wagner, "Aufgabe und Endziel des baukünstlerischen Schaffens," in *Handbuch der Architektur*, part 4, *Entwerfen, Anlage und Einrichtung der Gebäude*, half-vol. 1, *Architektonische Komposition*, 3rd ed. (Stuttgart: Arnold Bergsträsser, 1904), 8, my translation.

[4] August Thiersch, "Proportionen in der Architektur," in *Handbuch der Architektur*, part 4, *Entwerfen, Anlage und Einrichtung der Gebäude*, half-vol. 1, *Architektonische Komposition*, 4th ed. (Leipzig: Gebhardt, 1926), 77, my translation.

[5] Walter Gropius, "Statt einer Vorrede: Bauhaus-Chronik 1925/1926," *Bauhaus* 1 (December 4, 1926): 2, my translation.

Image, Substance, Façade

Kyle Dugdale

To walk the streets of the modern city with Hans Kollhoff is a prolonged exercise in architectural despair.

To encounter in his company a vertiginous façade that drops from dizzying heights only to terminate, at ground level, in a gutter that slides apologetically under the thinnest possible membrane of exterior cladding . . . to confront an architecture that is ostensibly built in stone but that presents to the city, at its most public exterior corner, the gaping seam of a failed half-inch caulk joint . . . to push, on a crowded city street, past surfaces so cheaply assembled as to register signs of having lost every battle with every stray wheel of every passing baby carriage . . .

This is not even to begin to leaf through the modern city's catalog of horrors: blankly glazed elevations that oscillate between exposing the embarrassment of material poverty within and reflecting the reality of visual anomie without; precast components, void of detail, designed to appear respectable at a minimum altitude of 100 feet but in fact installed at eye level, disfiguring the public space of the street; failed pedestrian arcades, set back from the street, into which no pedestrian will ever venture; newly-constructed exterior envelopes, recently photographed in all their paper thinness, betraying signs of decay before their retouched images have even been published; monuments to passing architectural fascinations that have aged prematurely, shedding every vestige of conceptual interest, yet doomed to linger on in the city for subsequent decades of accumulating tristesse.

The list of architectural misfortunes could be extended. And it is symptomatic of an endemic malaise. For if there is any common ground between Hans Kollhoff and Rem Koolhaas—who collaborated, several decades ago, on the rebuilding of Berlin—it can perhaps be found in a shared recognition of the junkspace that comprises the architect's modern city.

What differs is the response.

Kollhoff cares a great deal about how buildings are assembled, how they rise from the ground, how they meet the sky, how they expand and contract with fluctuations in temperature, how they age with the passing decades. He speaks of architecture's commitment—to the city, to the public, to the future—in terms that make it clear that such commitment must bear societal implications at the largest scale, and be reflected not only in architecture's immaterial promises but also in its material substance. Kollhoff cares about such substance a great deal—too much, perhaps, to guarantee glad acceptance within the insubstantial terms of contemporary building culture.

Substance over image, image over substance: a contest of almost moral dimensions. An architecture worthy of its name should, one might imagine, promote a certain correspondence between image

left Hans Kollhoff, former DaimlerChrysler Building, now Kollhoff Tower, Potsdamer Platz, Berlin, 1997–2000

and substance. After all, this is also a political matter of some significance.

So it is perhaps surprising that a studio taught by Hans Kollhoff could provoke allegations of façadism—presumably the antithesis of substance—while also generating such compelling images.

To be sure, Kollhoff's pedagogy pays close attention to the façade. It pays attention to the façade as a form of articulation that must struggle, in today's context, to preserve the expression of solidity, clarity, and dignity. Such attention requires the investment of time; and within the constraints of a single semester this comes at a cost. Not every aspect of the problem can claim to be equally resolved. But it is the differences between Kollhoff's pedagogy and that of his disciplinary peers that repay attention. Few studio instructors ask their students to study possibilities of exterior form before interior dispositions have even been broached. Few place such severe restrictions on material choices for exterior façades. Few demand such close attention to material thickness and jointing, or to their differing articulation at re-entrant and exterior corners. Kollhoff's pedagogy embodies a very specific set of convictions: the expression on the façade of the city cannot be an afterthought, and its materiality is not, it seems, a matter to be left to the free choice of the individual architect—or, for that matter, of the developer.

To be sure, Kollhoff is not alone in his attention to the façade. To study the products of New York City's recent experiments in the building of high-rise residential towers is to recognize that what separates a tower designed by Frank Gehry from a tower

above Josef Kaiser and Walter Franek, Karl-Marx-Allee 45, Berlin, 1964
left Peter Behrens, AEG Turbine Factory, Berlin, 1909

above *Miserables* graffiti, in courtyard behind Memhardstraße 8, Alexanderplatz, Berlin, built 1984 by Kollektiv Klaus Bläsing

designed by Robert A. M. Stern is not, primarily, the logic of its structural systems, the organization of its interior spaces, the planning of its vertical circulation, the standard of its amenities, or the ideology of its attitude to the ground plane of the city. This is not even to broach the subject of identity, of marketing, of image.

Yet Kollhoff recognizes that the boundary between image and substance deserves care. Easy distinctions are dangerous, as are moral pronouncements. Image cannot be dismissed out of hand as a thin shadow of substance. On the contrary, Kollhoff's students are typically asked to design the image as a means to studying the substance. In this instance, they were asked to produce interior renderings at an unprecedentedly early stage of the project, paying attention to issues that are elsewhere often relegated to being mere afterthoughts: lighting, furnishing, character. They were asked to produce large-scale charcoal drawings of their buildings' exteriors before the semester was even half-way through, crystallizing questions of formal coherence and studying the ways in which light plays across the solid surfaces of the city. They were asked to produce large-scale details that might illustrate an attitude to the way one piece of stone slides past another so as to emphasize thickness over thinness. They were asked to build analogue models of their towers at a massive scale, and then to produce photographic portraits of themselves standing next to their models, articulating the necessary embodiment of architectural vision. They were asked to invest in the image, just as they were asked to invest in the substance of the façade.

Such investment comes at a cost. It substitutes, in some cases, for a deeper engagement with the city's history, with the immediate urban context, and especially, no doubt, with that which frequently passes by the name of "conceptual interest."
But Hans Kollhoff is, quite frankly, disinterested in interest. The modern city of the architects, he insists, is bursting with architectural interest; but it is rarely well-built, seldom beautiful, almost never urbane. If confronted with a choice between the binary poles of Mies van der Rohe's distinction between the interesting and the good, Kollhoff's choice, too, is clear. It is also a choice that rejects an architectural trajectory that has led too often to an attitude of despair—an attitude that has not yet been banished from the modern city.

Projects

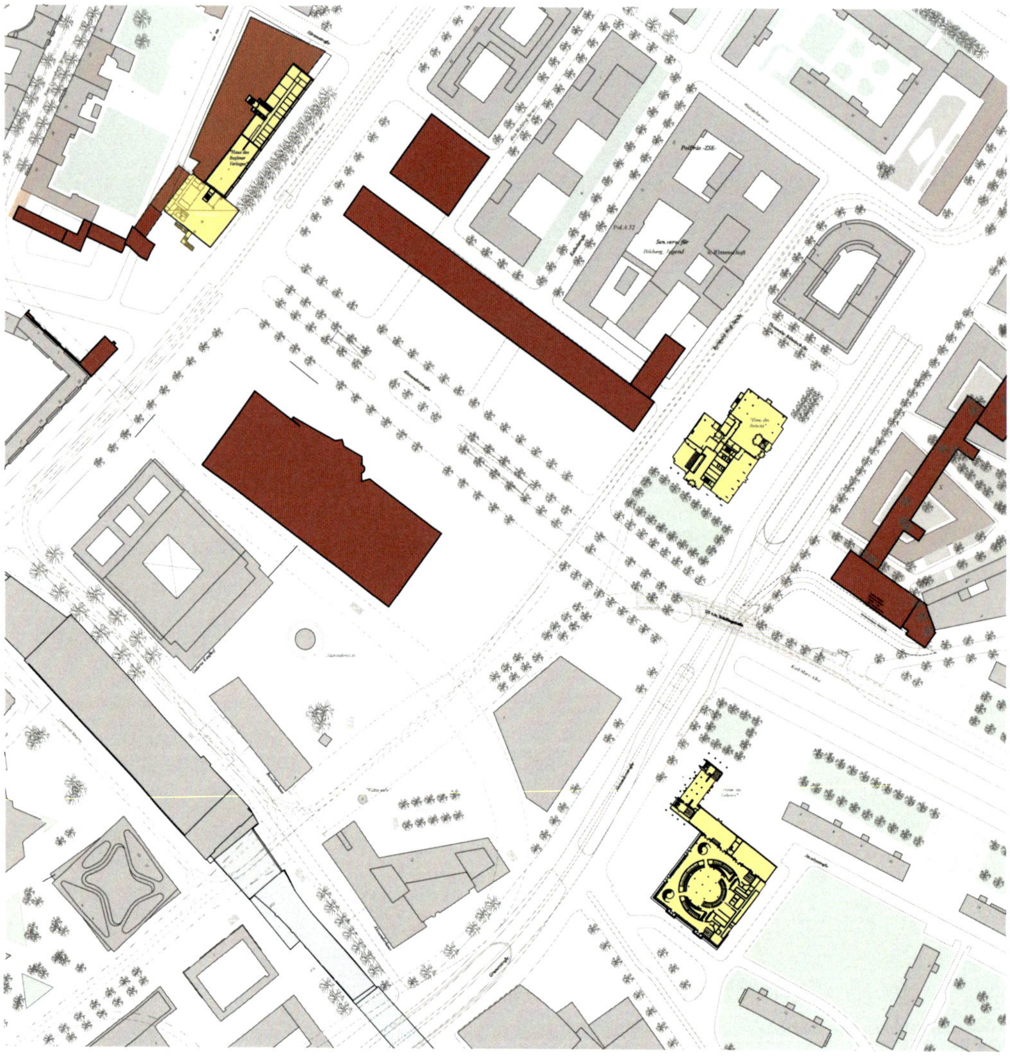

above and right Hans Kollhoff's 1993 master plan for Alexanderplatz reconfigured the urban square for a modern Berlin. The existing city layout (above) shows an urban quarter of vast, ambiguous spaces and monumental, wall-like buildings. Kollhoff's redesign (right) orders the city into navigable blocks and singular structures. Alexanderplatz itself regains prominence within a supportive context.

The studio placed each project on one of eleven unique sites within the Kollhoff master plan. Site dimensions, building limits, and tower positions remained faithful to the plan. Each project contended with its own localized urban brief and set of contextual issues while engaging a parallel exercise in scale, mass, and volume.

Past and Future

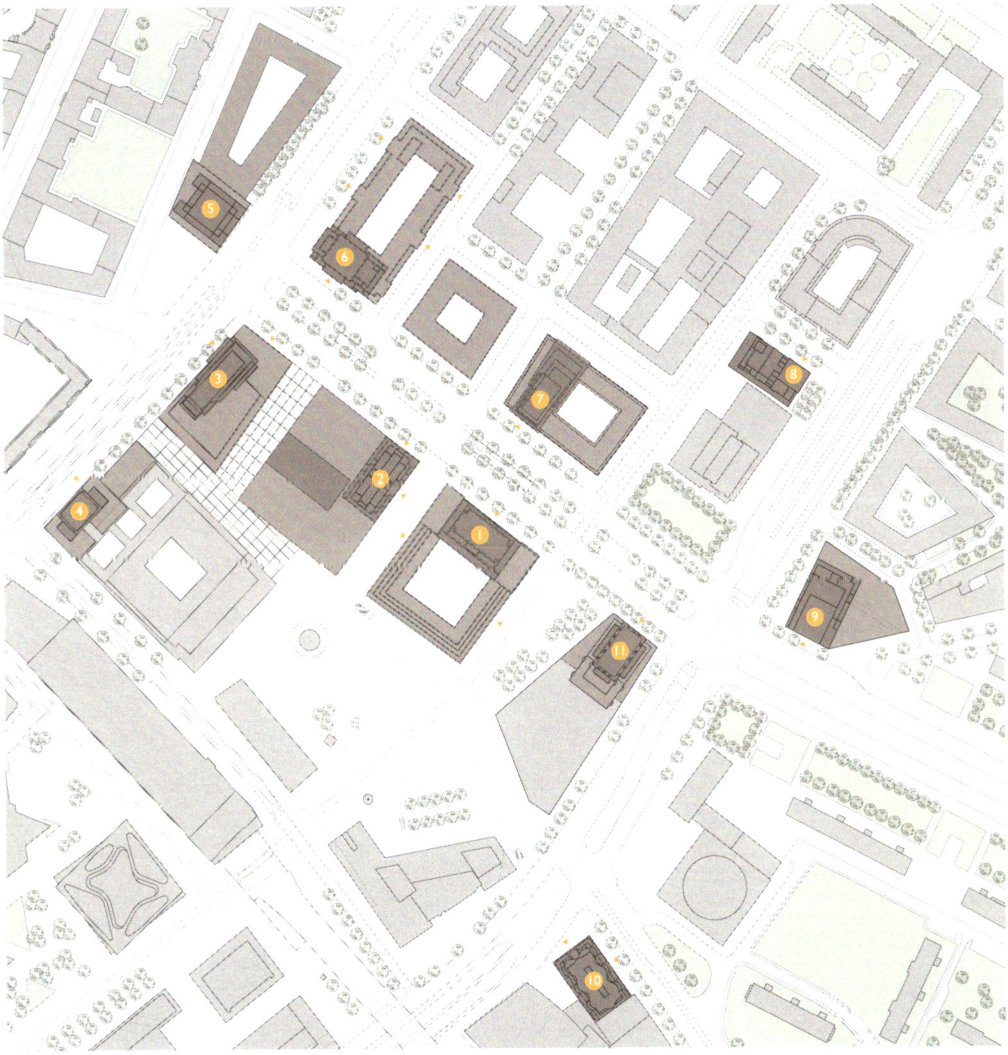

Existing buildings to be demolished	
Existing buildings to remain	
Proposed projects	

1 Dov Feinmesser
2 Gina Cannistra
3 Jason Kurzweil
4 Karl Karam
5 Eunil Cho
6 Richard Green
7 Kirk Henderson
8 Aymar Mariño-Maza
9 Yazma Rajbhandary
10 Megan McDonough
11 Ha Min Joo

01 Dov Feinmesser

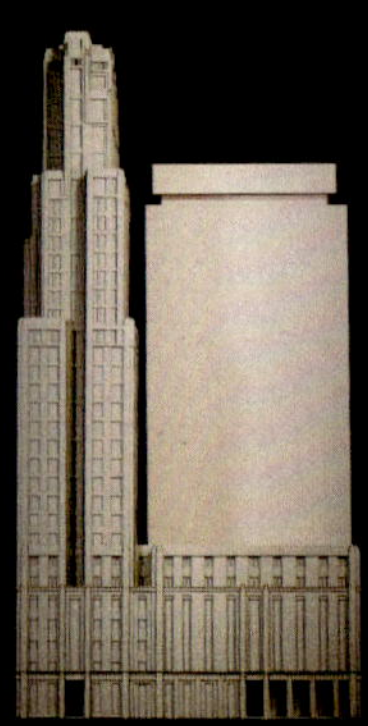

02 Gina Cannistra

03 Jason Kurzweil

04 Karl Karam

05 Eunil Cho

06 Richard Green

07 Kirk Henderson

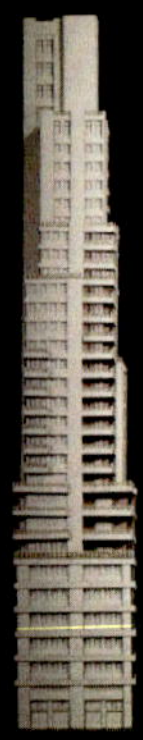

08 Aymar Mariño-Maza

09 Yazma Rajbhandary

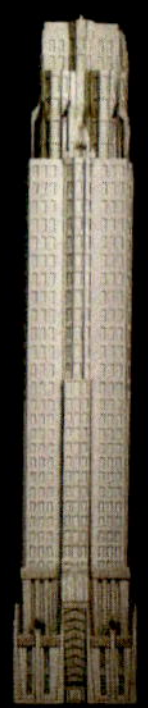

10 Megan McDonough

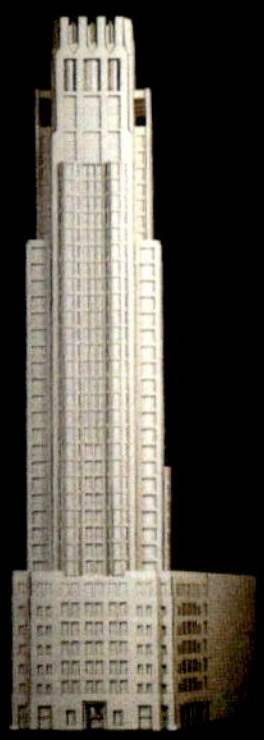

11 Ha Min Joo

Project Index

01 Dov Feinmesser

02 Gina Cannistra

03 Jason Kurzweil

04 Karl Karam

05 Eunil Cho

06 Richard Green

07 Kirk Henderson

08 Aymar Mariño-Maza

09 Yazma Rajbhandary

10 Megan McDonough

11 Ha Min Joo

01

Dov Feinmesser

"Who would not say?"

A provocation, a challenge, or simply a rhetorical statement? Its author Karl Friedrich Schinkel, whose shadow hung over this studio, might not have been surprised to find that in today's Berlin, as in cities around the world, residents are flocking to neighborhoods that seemed outdated shortly after the turn of the nineteenth century. Inspired by classically derived means of construction and articulation, the architecture of masonry and timber contributes to the formation of a unified but individually distinct fabric of low-rise residential buildings. It follows principles that seem to hold a universal appeal. Indeed, who would not say that the fabric of nineteenth- and early twentieth-century Berlin, Paris, or London has stood the test of time?

The tower, however, while an undeniable reality of the contemporary city, is not part of the image of this fabric, and in its gravity-defying rise, the question of appropriate architectural expression becomes critical if it is to relate to the successful urban fabric and its continuity. New York and Chicago offer, perhaps, some of the best examples of short-lived efforts to relate the two architectural vocabularies.

Hans Kollhoff argues that a classical tectonic, the relationship of building element to its construction and articulation, might be the appropriate medium through which to weave the fabric of the past into the expression of the tower and, by extension, the future of the city. Through this language, the relationship of exterior expression to interior space and the significance of tectonic in defining the *gravitas* of base and its sublimation into spire produce a grandeur and beauty of articulation that eclipse both designer and constructor.

The towers that constituted the formal artifacts of the studio addressed the needs and realities of a future focal point for the eastern portion of a revitalized Berlin. Conceptually, however, the studio challenged both the process of design and its responsibility to explore questions of fundamentals.

Thoughts of postwar East Berlin, of which Alexanderplatz was the center, steeped in myth and popular culture, evoke a stark and cold city under the thumb of a totalitarian regime in the guise of an egalitarian utopia. Upon reflection, this vision is not so dissimilar to that with which much contemporary architectural discourse celebrates the Modern and its influence in architecture. Steeped in such discourse, "Who would not say?" was the guiding principle; and these towers were our response.

left Charcoal perspective study

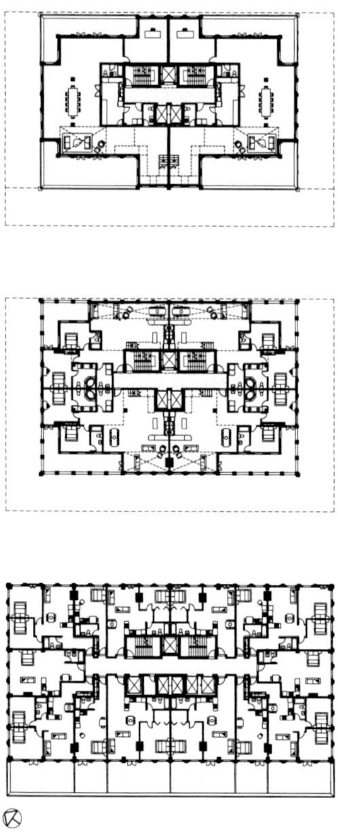

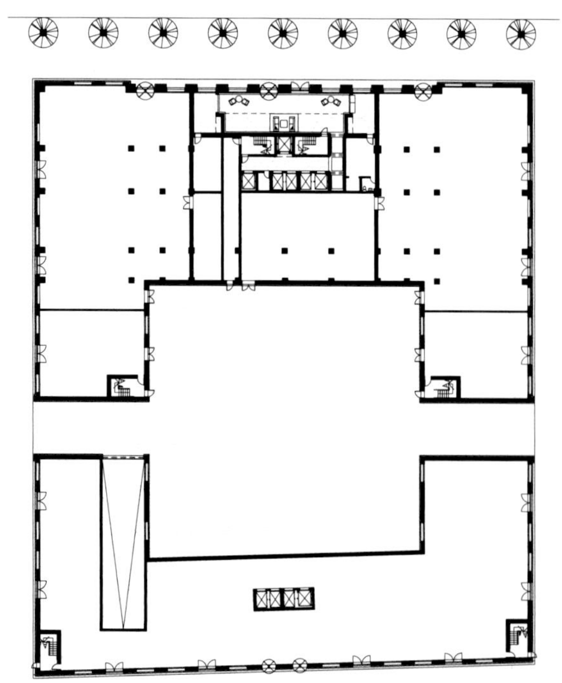

above Upper, intermediate, and lower residential level plans
right Ground level floor plan
above right Northeast elevation

top Penthouse, perspective rendering
above Entrance lobby, perspective rendering

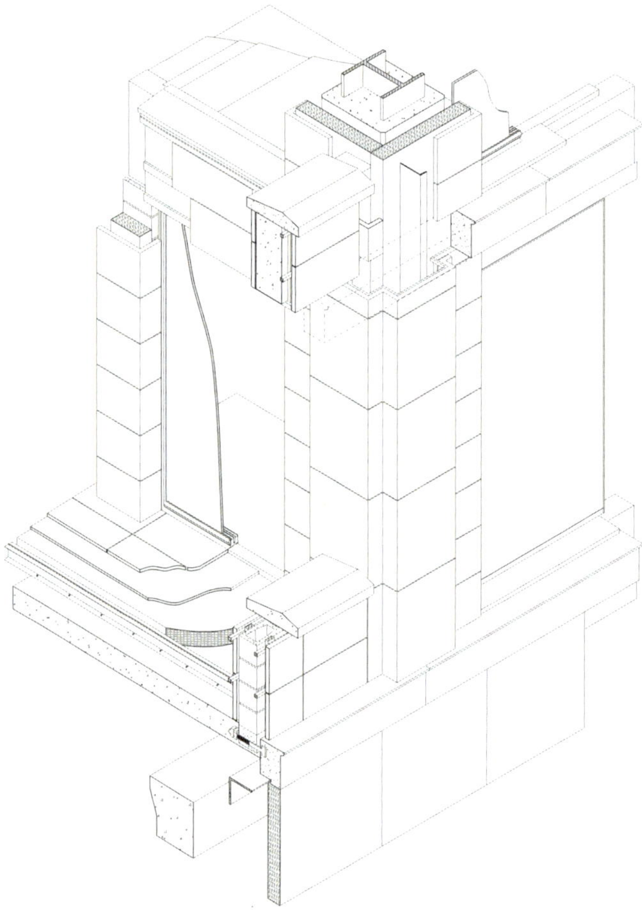

top Tectonic axonometric detail
above Large-scale model
opposite Perspective rendering

See also Assignment 4: Plan, Elevation, Perspective

02

Gina Cannistra

The complex history of Berlin can be traced through the developments and permutations of its residential buildings. Since its reunification, the city has experienced a significant housing shortage, and within that larger context Alexanderplatz has become a center of urban revitalization. This vibrant public square in the eastern part of the city has played a major role in its recent growth.

Hans Kollhoff's master plan for the area takes into consideration the human scale of the street and the history of the neighborhood. The newly defined streets are shaped by a series of mixed-use urban blocks, from which the residential towers rise, as if vertical extensions of the earth.

This project focuses on the architect's responsibility to the urban environment, the importance of tectonics, the current state of urban dwelling, and the future of the city of Berlin.

This new residential building aims to create a sense of identity for its residents through its siting and expression. The tower hugs the eastern corner of the site, offering both a slender contribution to the skyline at a prominent intersection along Alexanderstraße and a massing at the base that is respectful of the Behrens buildings that line the historic square. The project contributes to the civic realm by providing retail space, a public roof deck, and a porous ground floor with lounge and coworking areas. The tower's residential units maintain a relationship with the city regardless of their location within the building. Both circulation areas and residential units offer equal access to natural light, while the sizes of each floor's windows correspond to their elevation above the city. As the tower rises, mass gives way to transparency and to emerging terraces, which allow residents to engage more fully with the city below.

left Charcoal perspective study

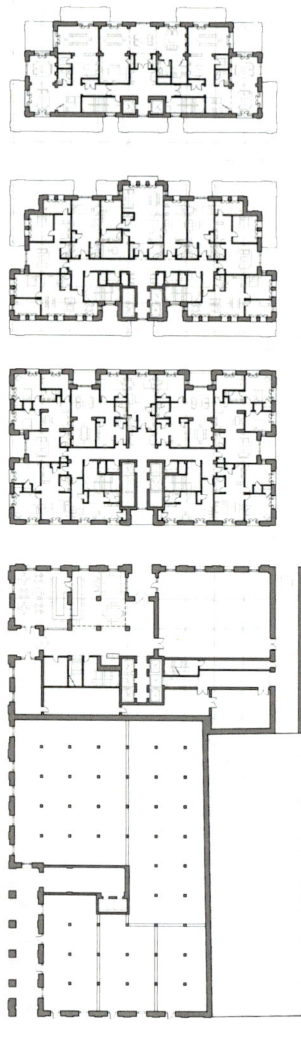

above left Alexanderplatz elevation
above right Upper, intermediate, and lower residential level plans, with ground level floor plan

above Entrance lobby, perspective rendering
above right, top to bottom Penthouse, one-bedroom, and studio apartments, perspective renderings

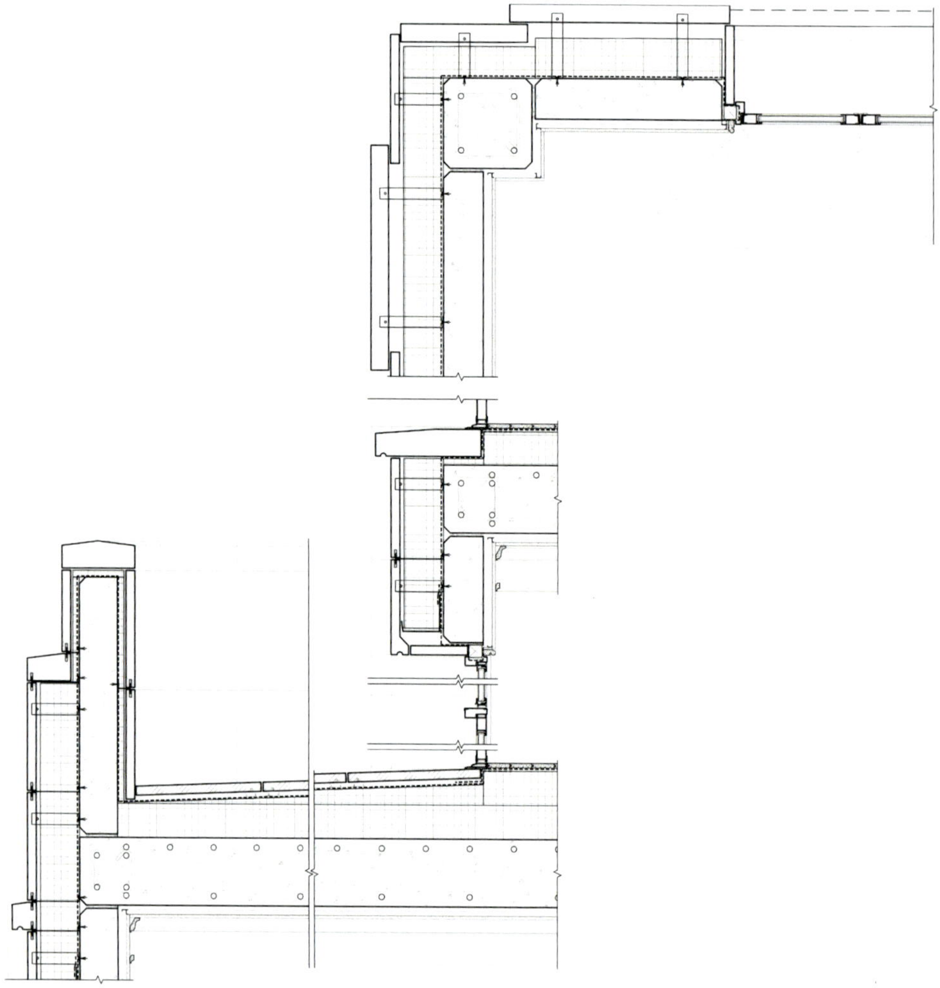

top Tectonic plan/section detail
above Large-scale model
opposite Perspective rendering

See also Assignment 6: Site, Core

03

Jason Kurzweil

Alexanderplatz, the de facto center of East Berlin, still preserves traces of East German socialism. Abandoned residential blocks are prime for transformation, and unapologetically wide boulevards await the grand military parades of May Day. Hans Kollhoff's master plan, tested in this studio, aims to humanize this aspirational district by introducing eleven new towers driven by a carefully crafted tectonic sensibility.

The studio's projects, though individually designed, play together within a greater ensemble. Kollhoff assumes the role of conductor establishing simple guidelines, articulating a shared commitment to public space and to architectural craft. The conversation between the towers creates a cohesive urban experience whose sum is greater than its parts.

This building negotiates three streets at once. Alexanderstraße is the primary boulevard addressed by the tower. It transitions into Münzstraße, a lower-scale street consisting of residential buildings and storefronts. The third, Karl-Liebknecht-Straße, is a bustling six-lane boulevard with a surface tramline running parallel to the project's broad face.

While the tower is at a much larger scale than the immediate context, the podium negotiates the intersection of unique street conditions. Windows, floor heights and storefronts work to soften the transition from the more intimate Münzstraße to the grand Alexanderplatz. An arcade above the street level serves as a transition between podium and superstructure, a nod to the neighborhood's consistent datum. The tower's stone-grey exterior approaches the Berlin sky, at times seemingly close at hand. Juliet balconies, set into the façade, invite the city into the units while maintaining order across the elevation. Finally, loggias mark the top of the tower's setbacks and offer moments for clouds and building to interact. The tower may be of the earth, but its aspirations are skyward.

left Charcoal perspective study

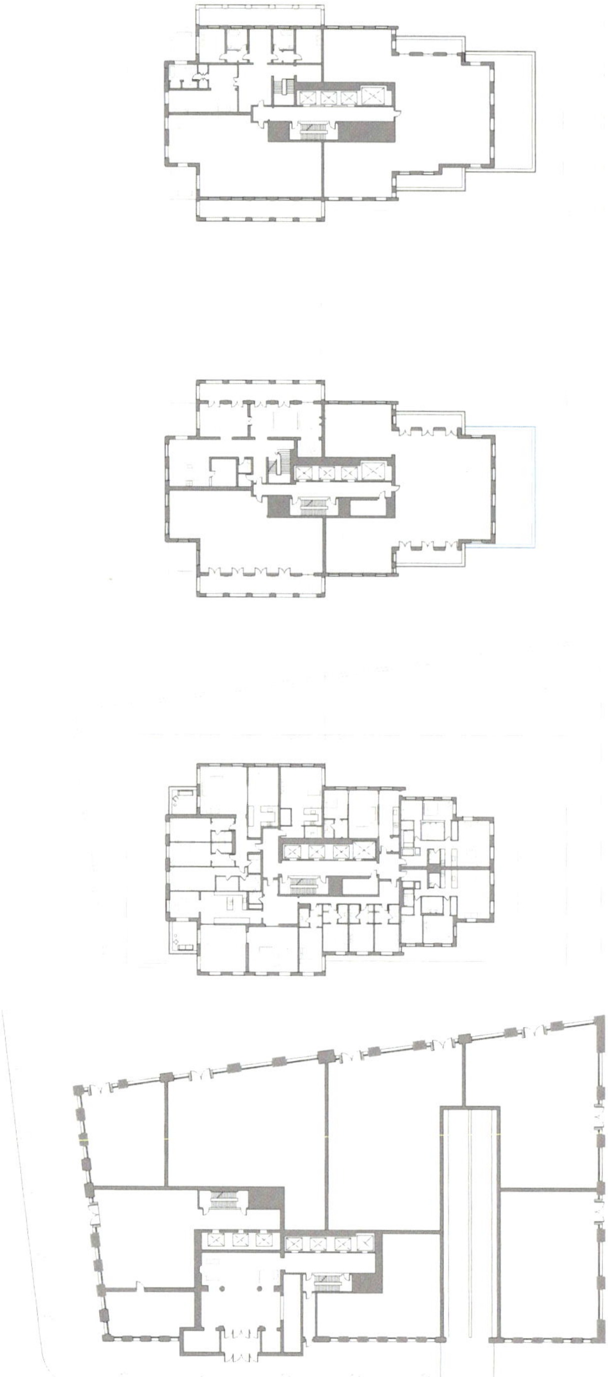

above left Upper, intermediate, and lower residential level plans, with ground level floor plan
above right Penthouse, market-rate one-bedroom, and studio apartments, perspective renderings
opposite Alexanderplatz elevation

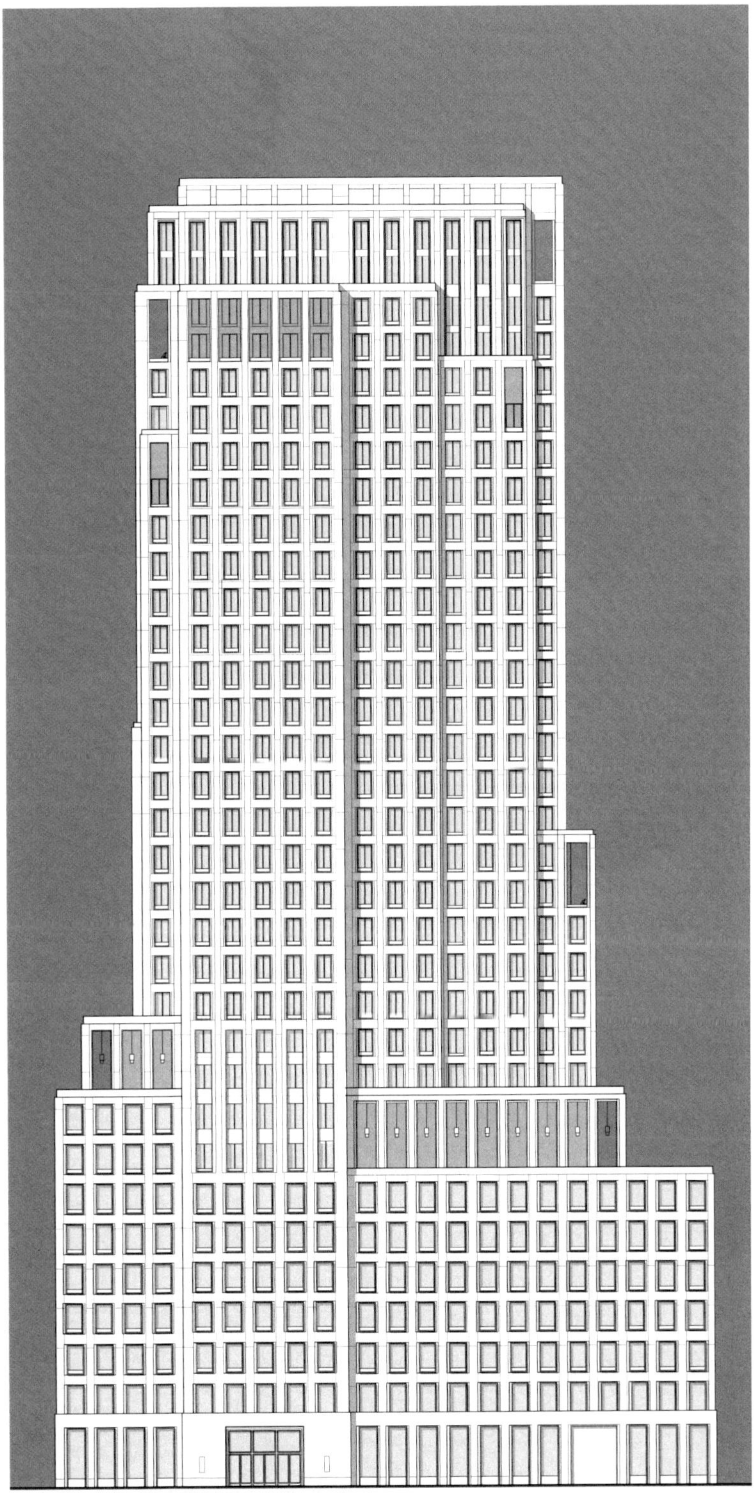

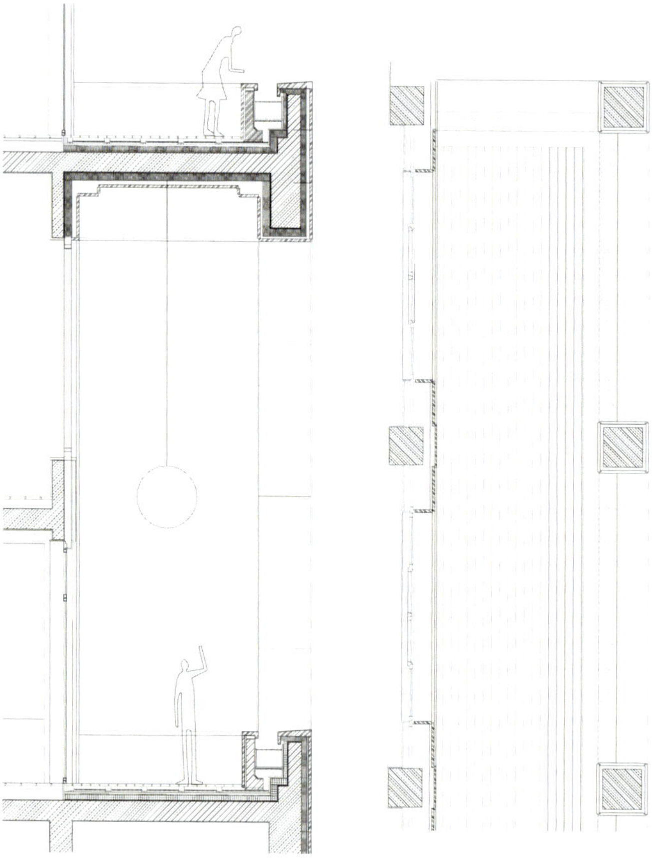

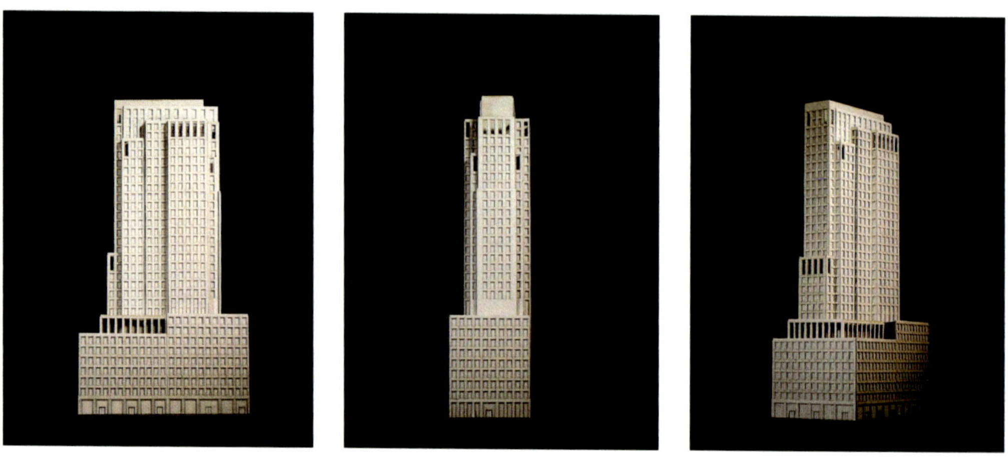

top Tectonic plan/section detail
above Large-scale model
opposite Perspective rendering

04

Karl Karam

The city of Berlin is spread across a wide area, planned for a population more than double its current size. The city needs density and friction, and place-making has proved challenging; but Alexanderplatz presents itself as offering that potential.

Overlooking Alexanderplatz, this tower aims to preserve the multiple microcosms that shape Berlin's renewed identity by offering a layered proposal that is capable of accommodating a variety of tenants with different lifestyles, needs and abilities. Located at a busy crossroads. It is a corner building that defines the edge between the street and the pedestrian area, while sitting over a busy train station that accommodates a constant flow of people and traffic. The tower announces the presence of Alexanderplatz, and each of its four façades is unique to what it faces. It addresses all four directions, shaped both by the city and by the site. The base provides a stepping-stone, a perforated block anchoring the tower to the ground while inviting pedestrians in through the street-level colonnade.

The transition that is visible in its façade is a product of composition of space, access to light, and adaptation to site-specific variables. Moving upward, the tension between light and shadow reveals the architecture's driving forces, shaping a narrative between ground and sky. The tower's façade opens as it rises—ending, finally, with the bare necessary structure and a fully transparent glass surface.

left Charcoal perspective study

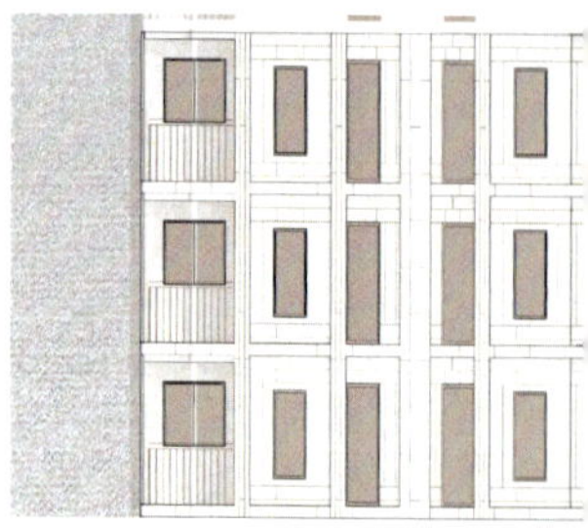

above left Karl-Liebknecht-Straße elevation
above right Upper, intermediate, and lower residential level fenestration details
opposite Luxury apartment, market-rate one-bedroom apartment, and lobby, perspective renderings

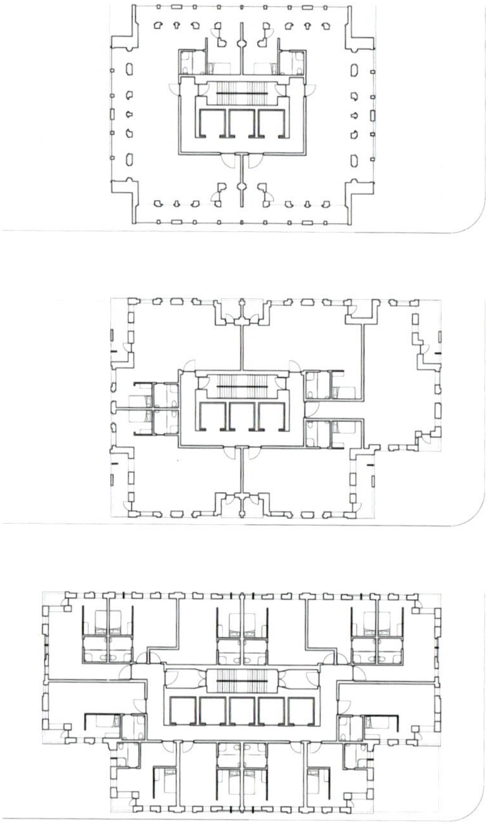

top Upper level floor plans
above Large-scale model
opposite Perspective rendering

05

Eunil Cho

This stone-clad residential tower is understood to be a vertical extension of the earth, rather than a constructed artifact to be dropped onto the ground plane. From overall expression to details of construction, it is to be interpreted as a monolithic whole, even if assembled from parts. This is the essence of what I learned from Hans Kollhoff: your home is where you feel attached to the earth.

The building is a tower with three exposed façades, designed for a complex site that must reconcile various disparate realities. It serves as a symmetrical terminus for the long axial approach of Karl-Marx-Allee/Alexanderstraße, but it must also negotiate the asymmetry of its disposition relative to other city streets, addressing an adjacent public space to the southwest, and abutting the site of the existing 1973 Haus des Berliner Verlags to the northeast.

At street level, a double-story base articulated in a darker stone offers covered access to discreet points of entry that separate commercial from residential access. Particular attention is given to the residential entrance lobby, the austerity of its limited color and material palette developed in a vocabulary that overlays sharp modern lines onto the generous volumes and geometries of a longer tradition. From its base, the tower rises in a series of carefully controlled steps; and as it does so, its floor plans grow progressively smaller, accommodating a variety of interior arrangements that in turn make possible a full range of programmatic uses and housing typologies.

left Charcoal perspective study

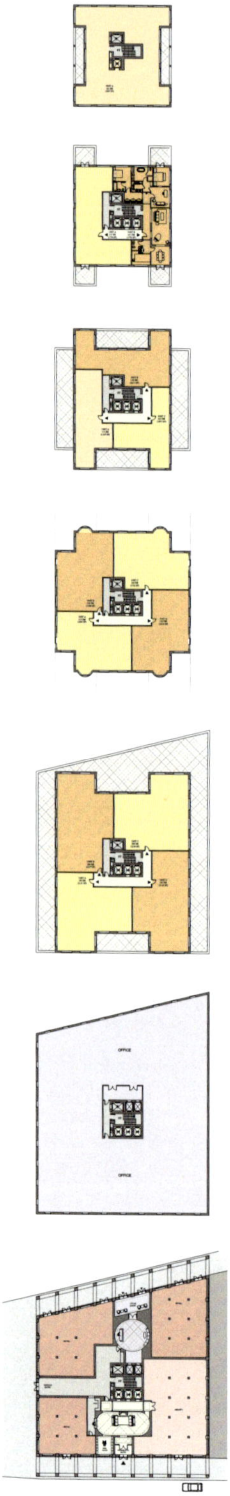

above Floor plans
above right "The 18th Floor," video short, 2:13 minutes

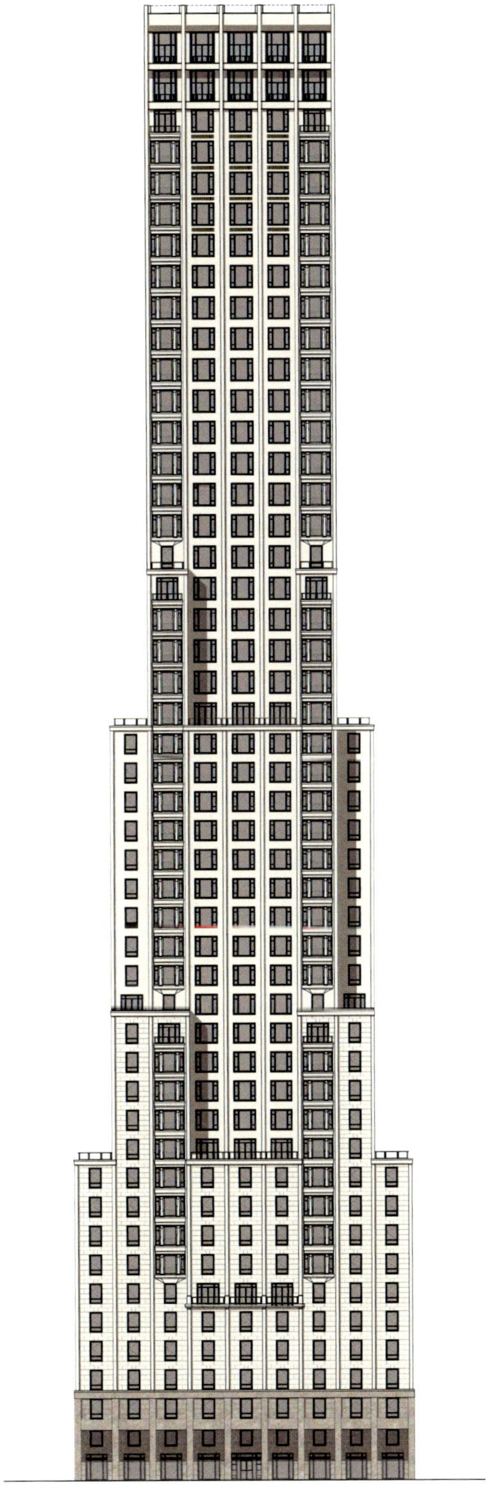

top left Luxury, market-rate one-bedroom, and studio apartments, perspective renderings
above Lobby, perspective rendering
above right Karl-Liebknecht-Straße elevation

top Façade plan, section, and elevation details
above Large-scale model
opposite Perspective rendering

06

Richard Green

Sited on a prominent corner along Berlin's kinked east west axis, the tower leans its heft toward this corner by superimposing an imbalanced, spiraling series of setbacks onto a balanced, cruciform massing. The resulting dynamism pushes the tower's vertical emphasis onto this critical corner.

At a finer scale, the façade continues this stressed verticality. The means of capping joints between prefabricated wall panels with additional stone elements evolves from a flush condition at the base, unifying the tower with its connected perimeter block, through to a deeper, layered form in the upper reaches, the leading face continuing in the same plane as at the ground. The remainder of each panel exhibits its assembly through carefully proportioned, layered stone elements around a uniform window. Such an arrangement within and between these panels expresses the tower's tectonic argument: it is an assembly of components which appear massive and heavily wrought at the connection with the ground, yet increasingly light as they reach toward the sky.

As the tower rises, its interior spaces also become increasingly open to their lofty setting. Above the solid base (housing active street-facing retail spaces and office floors), with simple windows puncturing the façade, the lower apartments of the tower inhabit the wall with Juliet balconies. Rising further, these develop into two-level inset balconies, conceived in section to maintain light and privacy to both floors without interrupting the external contour line of the tower itself. At the crown, volumes within the building's tectonic lattice are hollowed out to create covered terraces within the tower's overall form.

The consistency of window dimensions places the various units within a familial relationship, while the increasing spatial complexity of their relationship with the exterior wall and city beyond establishes a vertical hierarchy.

left Charcoal perspective study

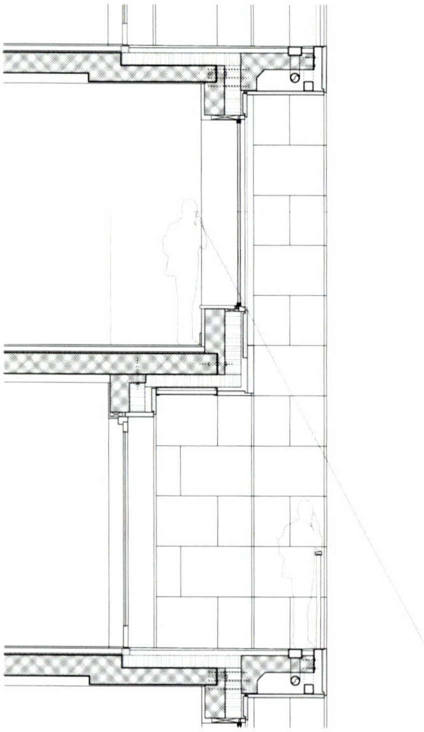

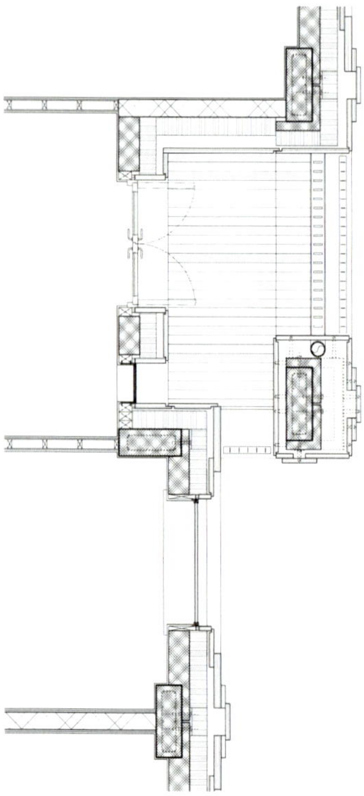

above Tectonic plan and section details
above right Alexanderstraße elevation

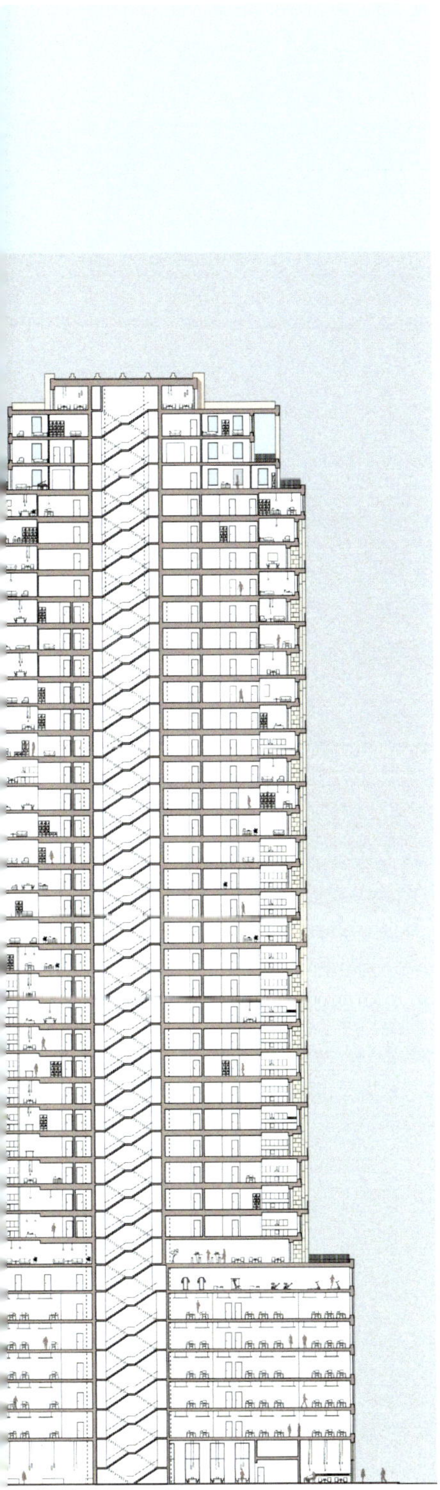

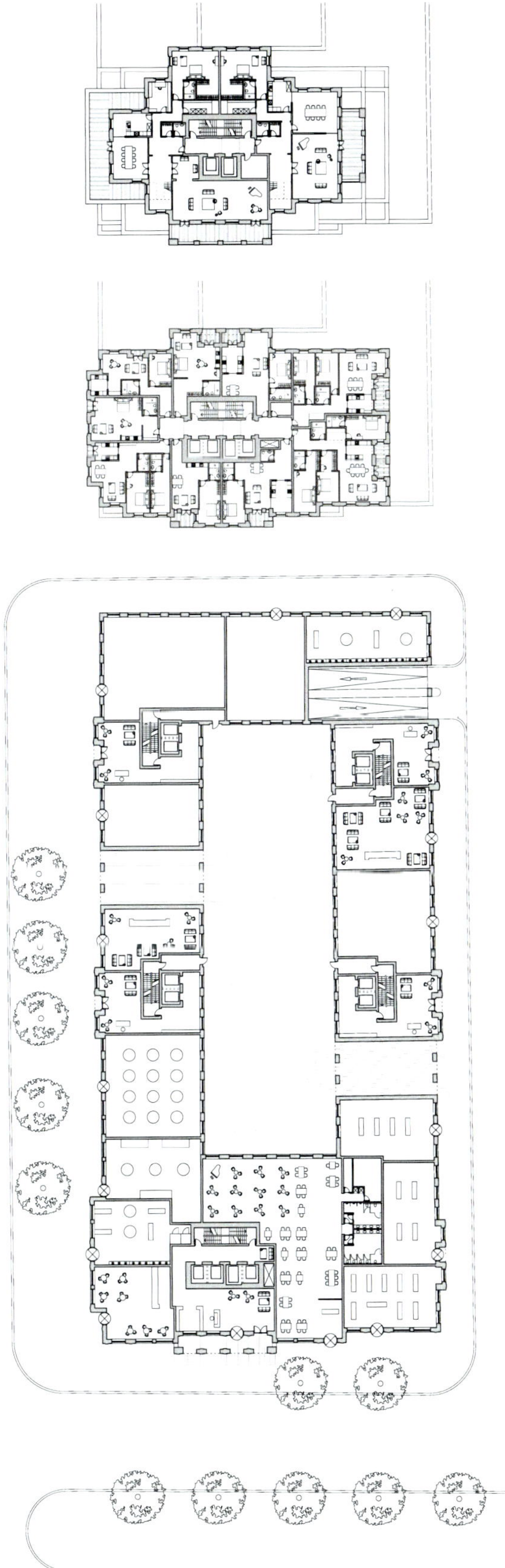

above Section
above right Upper, middle, and ground level plans

top left Exterior terrace, perspective rendering
top right Termination detail, sketch
middle right Lobby, perspective rendering
above Large-scale model
opposite Perspective rendering

See also Assignment 2: Living Room

07

Kirk Henderson

A site is not only an ecology of urbanity. First, it is square footage of fixed dimensions that determine the bounds of a future building. A façade is not only a haptic mediator between public and private. First, it is a feasible arrangement of solid building elements and windows in vertical planes. A balcony is not only a refuge of domestic liminality. First, it is a question of cold floors, and of how to treat the thermal bridge inherent in the structure of a cantilevered exterior slab.

In these and many other ways, the Kollhoff studio juxtaposed design theory with built and inhabited reality. Other studios inculcated analogy, allegory, and fantasy into our design pursuits. This studio asked instead for our visceral empathy with the unvarnished reality of objects, spaces, and buildings. In foreclosing our indulgent, tortuously premeditated narratives, it offered a grounded confrontation with architectural decision and consequence, resolved through the material of building itself.

This project reflects my own confrontation with this design ethic as much as it does a final resolution. I quickly became caught up in the building's form within the city. I thoroughly enjoyed the vintage novelty of our clay modeling exercises, and my thumbnail sketches tested overall figure and composition. The result was a good, high-level story based on massing and orientation: main entrance on the principal thoroughfare, hotel and amenities on the side. The tower offers strong verticality to counter the grandiose urbanity of Alexanderplatz, stepping back evenly toward the residential district of Prenzlauer Berg to the north. Slight angular shifts further diffuse the tower's aggressive northern aspect, yielding to surprise when a formal symmetry is finally observed from the front.

Yet the overall adjustments to massing and urban narrative would later overdetermine the façade, program, and inhabited space. The subjugation to overall form required exorbitant labor to extract a credible resolution within the authority of the massing. I liked the regular verticality of the building's façade, along with its opportunities for articulation. I liked the ground floor program and the particular but also meaningfully linked character of its spaces. And I liked the spaces of the apartments, which offer lights to discernable shelter and quietude. The studio taught me, however, that while these results may be attractive, I should understand them more as consequences than as ends in their own right. In this way, it suggested a certain design moral: unintentional authority may offer fortuitous but not reliably equitable outcomes.

left Charcoal perspective study

above left One-bedroom apartment and lobby, perspective renderings
above center Alexanderstraße elevation
above right Floor plans

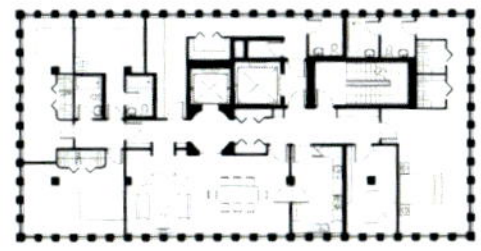

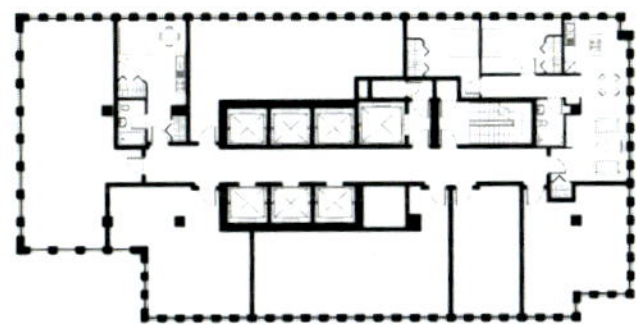

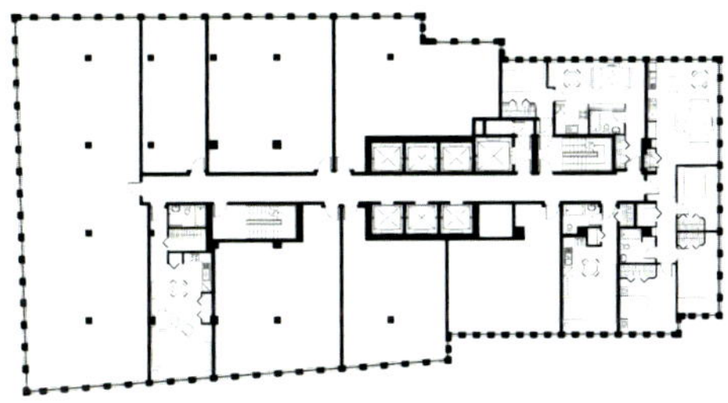

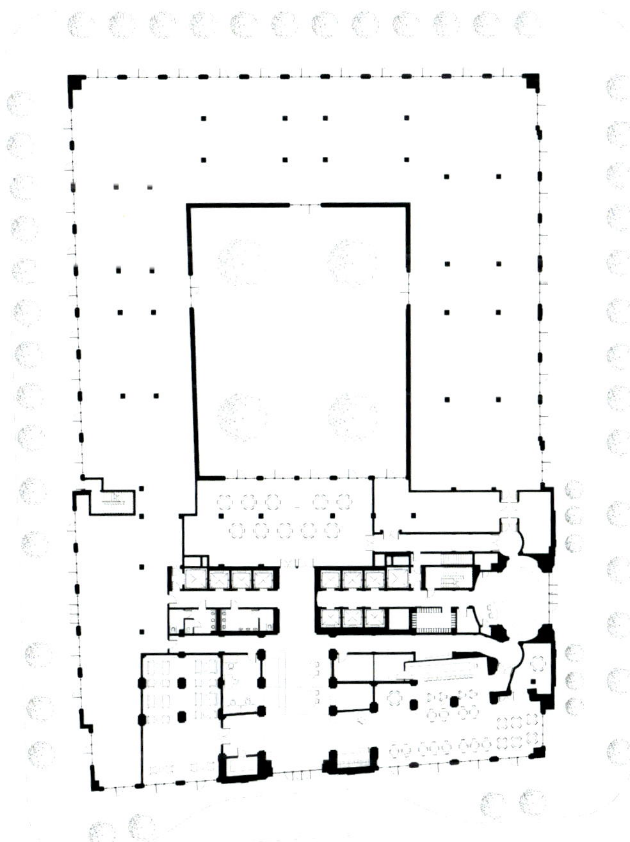

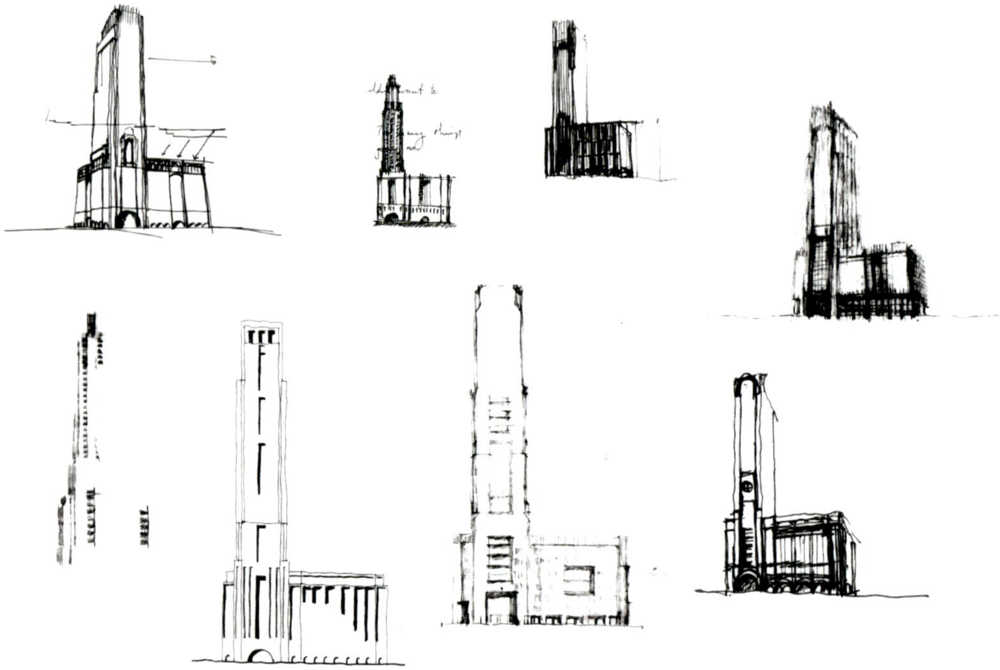

top Thumbnail sketches
above Large-scale model
opposite Perspective rendering

08

Aymar Mariño-Maza

Grandmothers leaning on kitchen windows, sheets strung on clotheslines, neighbors screaming across balconies, and young kids sneaking cigarettes on the fire escape. The inspiration for this apartment block is drawn from informal urban imagery as seen in small Mediterranean complexes in countries like Spain or Italy. But this is a high-rise in Berlin, not an apartment block in the Mediterranean. So, the project became about finding a way to create this interstitial setting within the social and climatic context of the site. East Berlin, with its complicated history and its sometimes-unforgiving climate, resists the social interactions that tend to develop in these informal outdoor in-between spaces.

The resulting architecture is an urban block that negotiates the transition from formal to informal through sectional cuts. These cuts, or slits, erode the solidity and stoic nature of the Berlin block required in the prompt. The slits create a series of neighborhood spaces, with interior balconies that face into the now semi-enclosed outdoor spaces. Through these slits, the overall form of the block pulls back from the street. The erosion is highlighted by the porous latticework, which serves as a shield from the wind, but also marks the private nature of the spaces that have been carved out of the block. From a solid street base to the interconnected apartments of the residential tower, the spaces transform not only formally but also socially, defining a distinctively intimate space of interaction.

left Charcoal perspective study

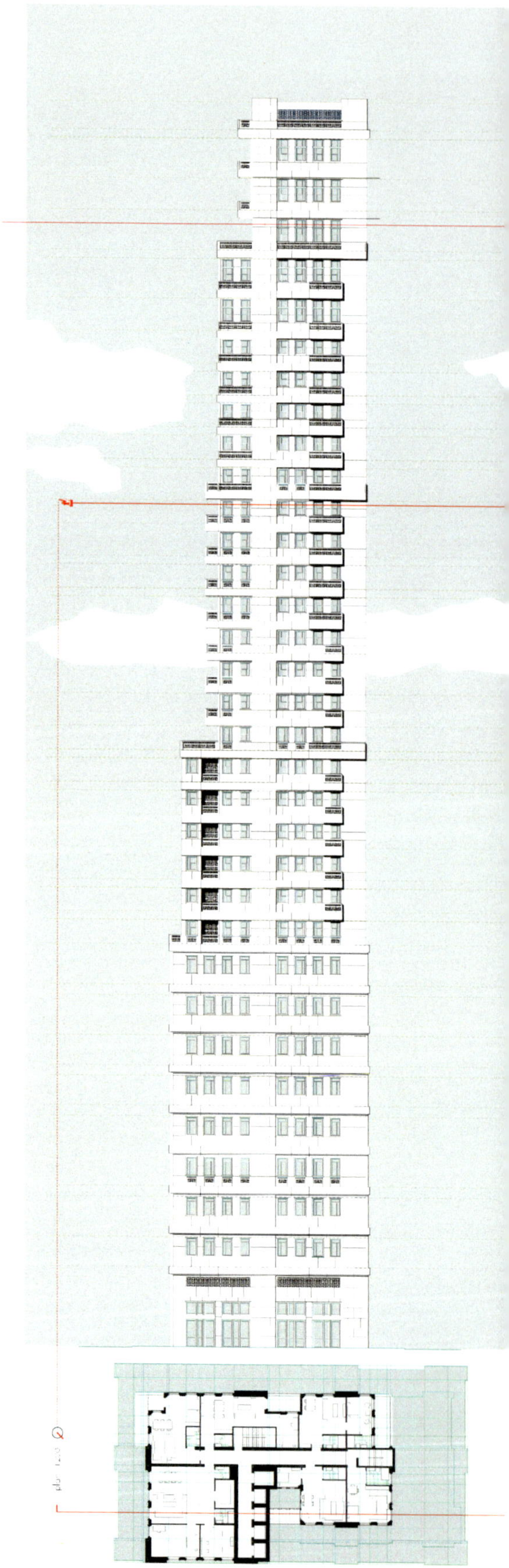

above Luxury, market-rate one-bedroom, and studio apartments, perspective collage studies
right Floor plans, section, and elevations

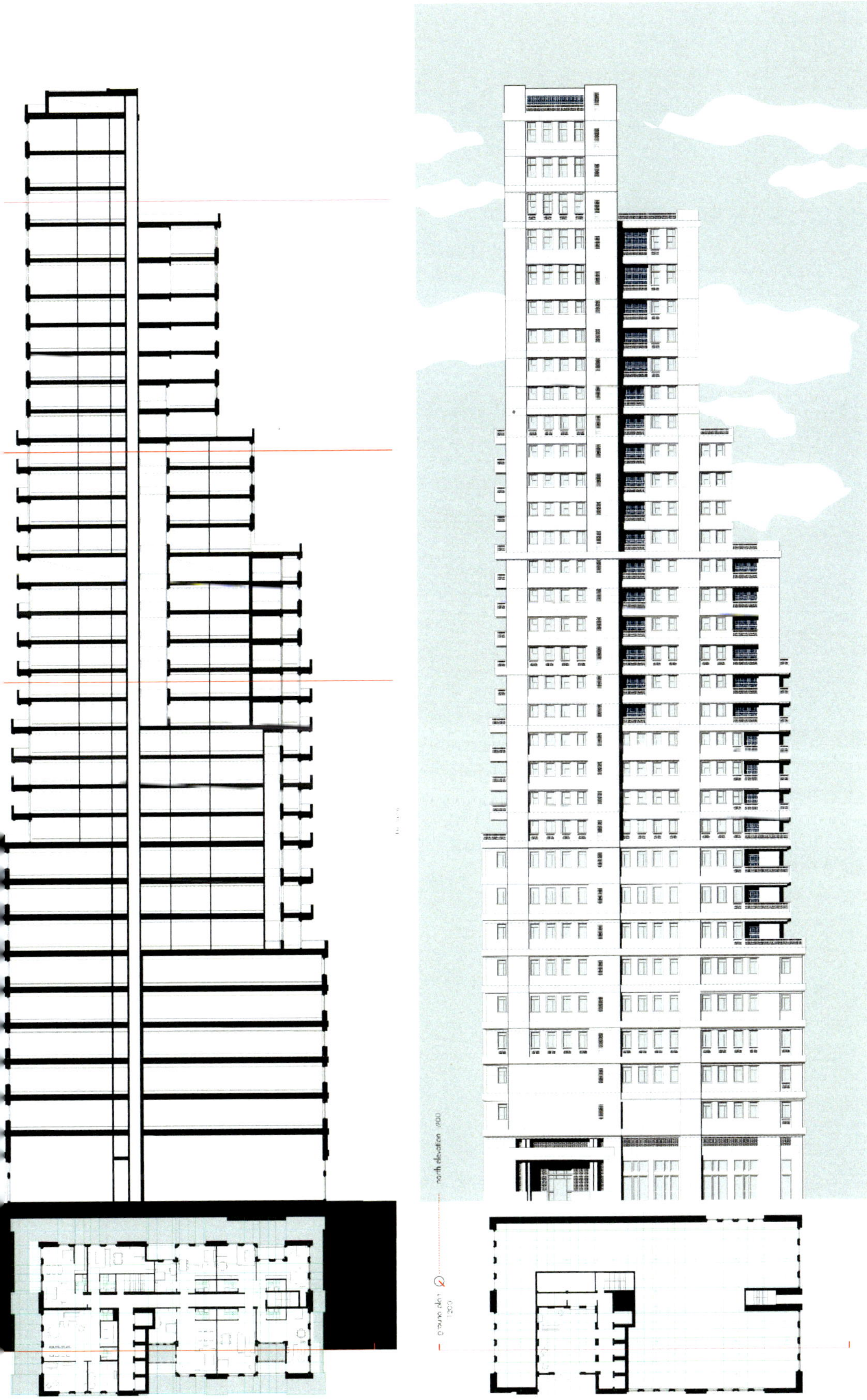
north elevation 1:200

top left Entrance lobby, perspective rendering
top right Fenestration collage studies
above Large-scale model
opposite Perspective rendering

See also Assignment 7: Tectonic

plans 1:200
luxury duplex

09

Yazma Rajbhandary

Hans Kollhoff's master plan for Alexanderplatz had two goals. The first was to humanize the imposing scale of streets such as Karl-Marx-Allee, so as to make the city more friendly to pedestrians. The second was to set specific material and dimensional standards for the surrounding towers, to create a unified neighborhood character of high-quality design. In 2016, much of Kollhoff's winning plan remained unimplemented. The studio brief presented this as a challenge. Working from the master plan, the goal was to redefine the urban blocks through tower and base structures designed within the modern context.

Situated at the intersection of the monumental Karl-Marx-Allee and Otto-Braun-Straße, this tower adopts the guidelines of the studio to complement the dimensions and qualities of the site. The building comprises the entire block, anchoring the site at the northeastern corner, where the tower is articulated as the most solid element in the design. This serves not only to restate the solidity of the tower, but also to define the urban street edge. The structure grows lighter as it rises and as the interaction between "inside" and "outside" becomes more pronounced, with apartments shifting from smaller studios to larger luxury units.

In conjunction with a well-articulated program focused not only on concept but also on experience, the tower's design tectonic points toward an enduring architecture that remains focused on serving the society for which it is built.

left Charcoal perspective study

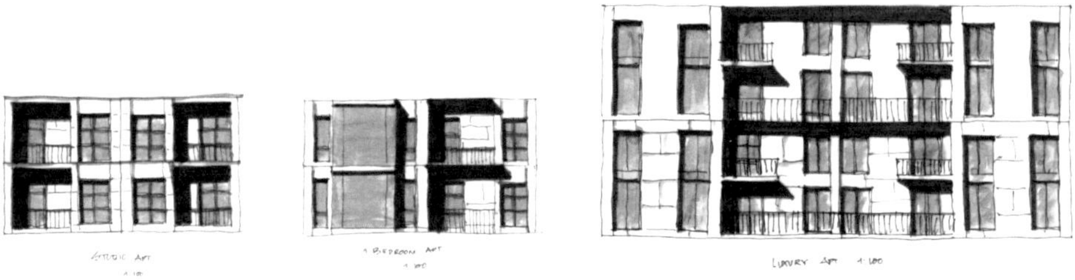

top Studio, one-bedroom, and luxury apartments, elevation studies
above Elevations

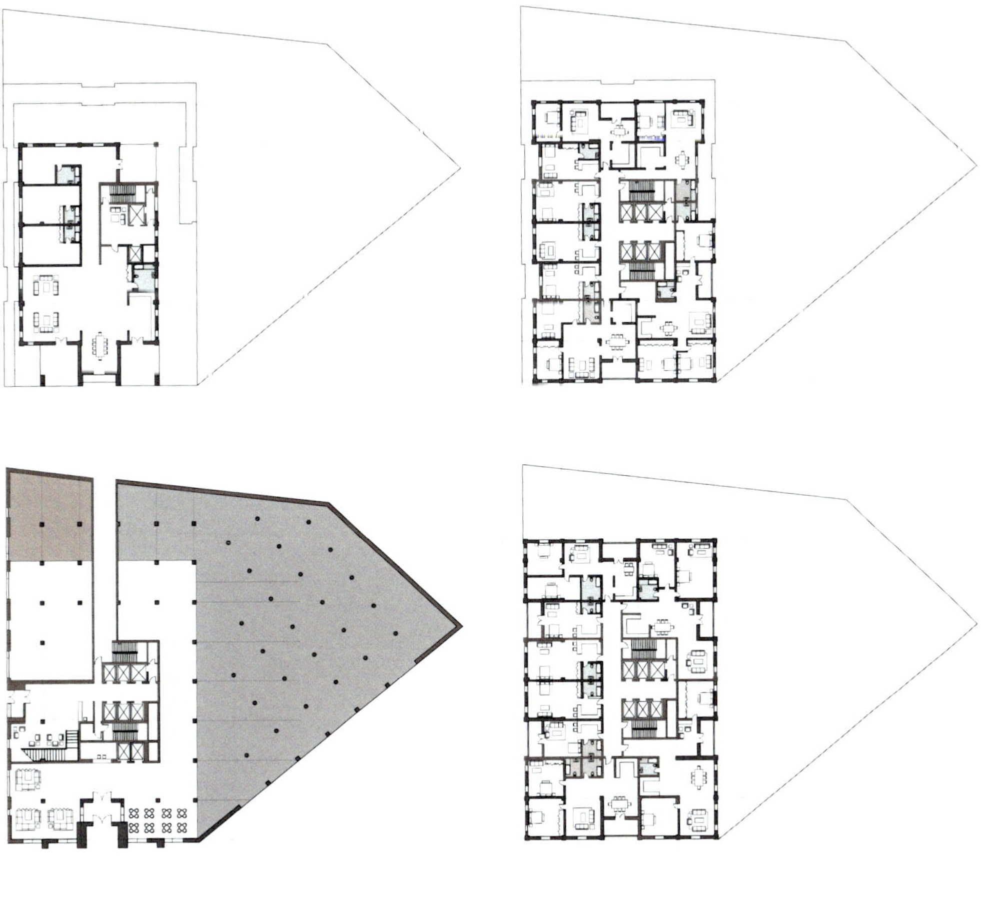

top Entrance lobby, perspective rendering
above Floor plans

top One-bedroom and studio apartments, perspective renderings
above Large-scale model
opposite Perspective rendering

10

Megan McDonough

As post-war housing blocks overtook Berlin, the integrity of the public street was lost. While striking in aerial perspective, massive purist forms and overly-wide public spaces tore apart the old, tightly-knit city and streets as effectively as air raids had done only years prior.

This studio argued against the concept that any building in a city could presume to behave autonomously. A building, and especially a tower, bears a responsibility to the street and to the public. In East Berlin especially, post-war housing developed according to a logic that was alienating to the pedestrian. The massively oversized Karl-Marx-Allee anticipates a parade that occurs one day a year but otherwise remains empty of social interaction. Strictly unornamented exteriors provide no relief from the vast expanses of concrete walls. Efficiency overrules architectural tradition.

The Soviet elite who championed the new cityscape were the very ones who elected instead to live in the (now rare) older masonry buildings. These structures achieved what the new could not, addressing the public with stoops and shops at street level, and with ornamental elements breaking down the scale of the floors above. The pattern holds true today, with the oldest architecture in high demand.

This particular tower marks an edge of Alexanderplatz as it beckons toward the open expanse to the east. It develops out of the folded language of the bay window—an element which allows inhabitants to partake simultaneously in the life of the street and in the privacy of their own living room. The bay increases in its divisions as the towers rise to a crenulated peak. A robust base houses a bank with a highly ornamented entrance sequence and enough visual weight to support a stone assembly. The new public corner contrasts vividly with the interiorized 1980s shopping center adjacent to the site. The ornament continues up the face of the tower, emphasizing tectonic logic, projecting skyward energy, and offering human-scale relief to the experience of the street. A public restaurant and bar grace the buttressed top, providing a viewing terrace out to the city and a reminder that the tower is but a piece of the urban fabric.

left Charcoal perspective study

above Elevations

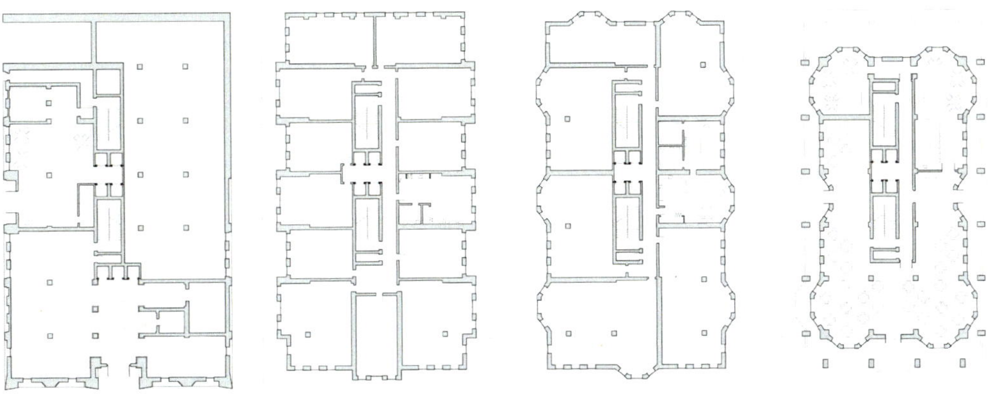

top Elevation ornament studies
above Floor plans

top Penthouse apartment, perspective rendering
above Large-scale model
opposite Perspective rendering

11

Ha Min Joo

This studio began with a strong foundation in the idea of *Tektonik*. The design process emphasized both the urban context and the concept of tectonics, with architecture interpreted as a monolithic whole, a solid mass created from the earth. Formal expression and physical materiality became the main instruments in understanding this notion of *Tektonik*, adopted as a guiding principle for design decisions. It is *Tektonik* that differentiates this structure from the prevalent glazed vocabulary of contemporary towers.

The most fundamental challenge was to create a monolithic structure from a series of stepped setbacks, demonstrating a sense of gravity with a firmly grounded base and a more delicate crown reaching toward the sky. The monolithic nature of the form was then articulated with solid corners and transparent centers to emphasize the verticality of the façade and to connect the base to the top. This also reintroduced the traditional tripartite composition of the façade, recognizing the historic context of East Berlin.

The unique site and the process of designing both inside-out and outside-in led to an exploration of the balance between the public and the private realm. Alexanderplatz is a public open space, with these residential towers as constitutive components. The building is located at a tip of the triangular retail block, with its individual units responding to their surroundings and establishing a close relationship between public and private.

left Charcoal perspective study

This project followed a rigorous design process, in which individual units and residents' experiences were contemplated first. It established the basic components of the building; but more importantly, it influenced the tower's visual expression by introducing bay windows and determining the relationship between glass and limestone in support of its overarching form and articulation.

The idea of the building as a vertical extension of the earth is not only a principle for creation of form, but also a commitment to the city and its surroundings. It demands that the building be cognizant of the history and character of the city, entering into a closer relationship with them. This building takes cues from the architecture of East Berlin in its proportion, composition, and articulation. With an emphasis on tectonics and on the balance between public and private, it aims to re-think tradition and historic character in the contemporary context.

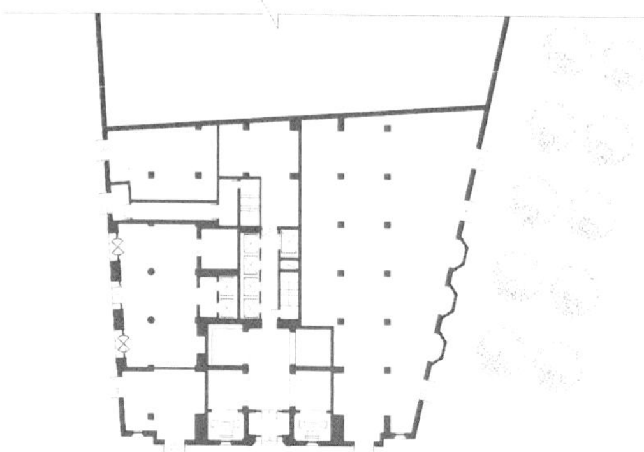

top Elevations

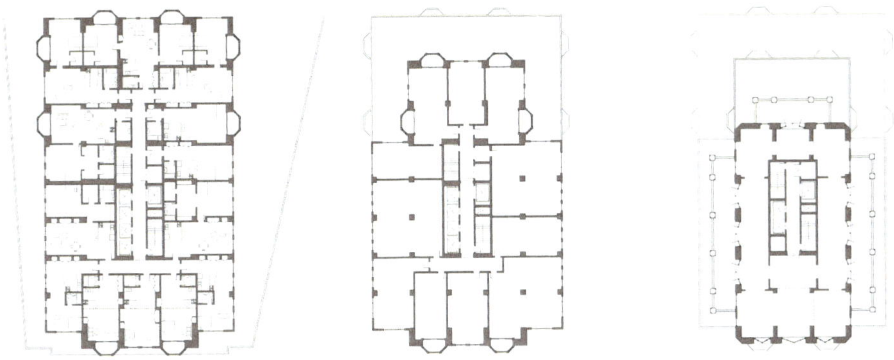

top Entrance lobby, perspective rendering
above Floor plans

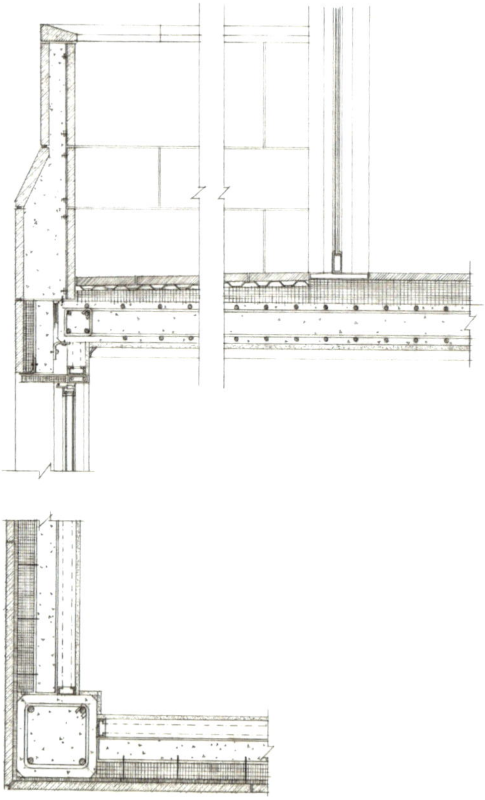

top left Tectonic plan and section details
top right Luxury, market-rate one-bedroom, and studio apartments, perspective renderings
above Large-scale model
opposite Perspective rendering

Participants

above In front of Karl Friedrich Schinkel's Altes Museum, Berlin, built 1823–30

Students

Gina Cannistra, now Gina Zari, graduated in 2017 and is a registered architect and associate at HBRA Architects in Chicago.

Eunil Cho graduated in 2016, taking a position with Hart Howerton in New York City. He is now project director at Rios in Los Angeles.

Dov Feinmesser graduated in 2016 and is now a project architect at Newman Architects in New Haven and a lecturer at Yale School of Architecture.

Richard Green graduated in 2017 and worked for Povero & Company in New York City, where his projects aptly included a tower and block development in Fargo, ND. He has since returned to London to work for De Rosee Sa.

Kirk Henderson graduated in 2016 with a joint MArch and MBA, taking a position with Harley Ellis Devereaux in Los Angeles.

Ha Min Joo graduated in 2017 and is practicing with Hart Howerton in New York City.

Karl Karam graduated in 2016 and is founding partner of Archave, based in Beirut, Lebanon.

Jason Kurzweil graduated in 2016 and took a position with Skidmore, Owings & Merrill in San Francisco. He has guest-lectured at Academy of Art University.

Aymar Mariño-Maza graduated in 2017 and worked for HBRA Architects in Chicago. Appointed H. Allen Brooks Fellow of the Society of Architecture Historians, she is currently consulting for the Inter-American Development Bank.

Megan McDonough graduated in 2016. She is a project architect with Houser Walker Architecture in Atlanta and a studio critic at Georgia Tech School of Architecture.

Yazma Rajbhandary graduated in 2017. She is now CEO of Kalap Architects in Kathmandu, Nepal, and has held a position as lecturer at Kathmandu Engineering College.

top
Ha Min Joo, Kirk Henderson, Aymar Mariño-Maza, Yazma Rajbhandary
middle
Megan McDonough, Eunil Cho, Jason Kurzweil, Richard Green
bottom
Gina Cannistra, Dov Feinmesser, Karl Karam

Kyle Dugdale is a critic at Yale School of Architecture, where he has taught history/theory and design since 2009. He is an alumnus of Yale's PhD program in architecture.

Faculty

Hans Kollhoff founded his Berlin-based practice in 1978 after completing studies at Cornell under Colin Rowe and Oswald Mathias Ungers. He taught for many years at the ETH in Zurich and continues to practice with Helga Timmermann.

above Hans Kollhoff, with Megan McDonough, in Berlin
opposite Kyle Dugdale, in Berlin

Jury

The Kollhoff Studio would like to thank all those jurors who offered their time and input, even in the face of vigorous disagreements. This includes Ioanna Angelidou, Thomas Beeby, Eve Blau, Karla Britton, Melissa DelVecchio, Judith DiMaio, Frank Gehry, George Knight, Barbara Littenberg, Daniel Lobitz, Michael Manfredi, Helga Timmermann, and Anthony Vidler.

above and opposite Final review, Rudolph Hall, New Haven

Acknowledgments

Dean Robert A. M. Stern, Dean Deborah Berke, and Publications Director Nina Rappaport provided invaluable support both for the studio and for the subsequent publication of this book. The smooth coordination of the studio itself was also thanks in no small part to Helga Timmermann. Fritz Neumeyer offered his expertise on the domestic architecture of Mies van der Rohe in Berlin, and Andrew Alpern offered his expertise on the residential towers of New York City. The editors are grateful also to the Central Archive of the Staatliche Museen zu Berlin for access to materials in the Karl Friedrich Schinkel archive, and to the staff of Haas Family Arts Library Special Collections for reference access to the eleven volumes of *The Mies van der Rohe Archive*. Richard DeFlumeri negotiated access to Rudolph Hall's Nalle Drawing Studio for the creation of the studio's large-scale charcoal drawings. To these and to other individuals who contributed along the way, the studio participants are deeply grateful.

It is not a question of preserving a bygone world in architecture but of taking care not to simply abandon values arbitrarily.

And yet that is precisely what early Modernism had to do in order to make itself heard. . . . So those who committed the great mistake were not so much the representatives of early Modernism, who had to be provocative, but those who uncritically picked up on their ideas in the fifties as if nothing had happened in the meantime and who to this day with boundless naivety think they have been clever if they, as modern architects, use glass and steel and paint their buildings white.[1]

[1] Hans Kollhoff, "Es geht nicht darum, eine vergangene Welt zu konservieren" [1993], trans. Chris Charlesworth, in *Kollhoff: Examples*, by Annegret Burg (Basel: Birkhäuser, 1998), 185. Originally published in *Centrum: Jahrbuch Architektur und Stadt* 4 (1993): 49–55.

opposite Hans Kollhoff, former DaimlerChrysler Building, now KollhoffTower, and Helmut Jahn, Sony Center, both Potsdamer Platz, Berlin, 2000

Colophon

This book follows YSOA standards established by MGMT. design studio.

Type is set either in Carol Twombly's Adobe Caslon Pro, based on William Caslon's eighteenth-century roman, or in a digital version of New Haven native Frank Hinman Pierpont's 1926 Monotype Grotesque, itself based on a typeface issued by Berlin's Berthold Type Foundry.

Colors used for endpapers and separating pages range from the standard traffic yellow (RAL 1023) of Berlin's public transit system to the blood orange (RAL 2002) of the U2 subway line that passes under Alexanderplatz.

Unless noted otherwise, all photographs are by studio members.